SATAN WANTS ME,

GOD HAS ME.

By Pastor Cora Grace (Kirby) Goldman

Copyright © 2009 by Pastor Cora Grace (Kirby) Goldman

SATAN WANTS ME, GOD HAS ME.
by Pastor Cora Grace (Kirby) Goldman

Printed in the United States of America

ISBN 978-1-60791-423-5

All rights reserved solely by the author. The author guarantees all contents are original and do not infringe upon the legal rights of any other person or work. No part of this book may be reproduced in any form without the permission of the author. The views expressed in this book are not necessarily those of the publisher.

Unless otherwise indicated, all scripture references come from the Authorized King James version of the Bible, copyright © 1985, published by C.D. Stampley Enterprises, Revelation Seminar.

www.xulonpress.com

DEDICATION

First of all, I dedicate this book to God my Father, Jesus Christ my Brother, and to the Holy Spirit, my Director. Without them, I would be dead. Thank You for loving me when it seemed no one cared.

To Pat Martin, to my granddaughter, Shannon Goldman Russel, to Pastor Rick Alcaraz and Johnathan Statan.

To my dear, sweet mother, who gave me life.

To my father and his battles.

To my children, whom I have learned so much from.

To my church people and the Appalachian Mountain people, who are more love than any biological family.

A special thanks to Michelle Levigne for her patience and putting all the finishing touches in place.

To Whom it May Concern:

I wish to introduce to you the ministry of Cora Goldman. I have never seen anyone with any greater heart and love for ministering to the needs of hurting people. Cora's compassion for the impoverished, bound, afflicted, and oppressed is evident by the way God uses her to serve people. Having been delivered from the deception of the occult, Cora Goldman has a heart to see people set free from Satan's lies and become aware of who they are in Christ.

You'll be blessed as you meet Cora and hear the burden of her heart, and I know she'll be an encouragement to congregations as she encourages them to serve God by serving others.

With His Love Compelling Us,

Pastor Daniel G. Skirvin
M-46 Tabernacle

* * * * *

To Whom it May Concern:

I have known Cora Goldman for many years and am familiar with the wonderful work she has done in founding "God's Mission Outreach." Cora is of excellent character, and has a rare and unusual heart to help others in her community as well as the people of Appalachia.

I understand that Cora has applied through the McDowell County Board of education for the Switchback School. In granting her request to consider "God's Mission Outreach" for this building, you will have played a major part in the betterment of her community.

Cora Goldman has struggled for 18 years to provide a much-needed service to those less fortunate and the acquisition of this building will certainly make the work easier for Cora and her many helpers.

Sincerely,

Alan L. Cropsey, Senator
33rd District
The State of Michigan

* * * * *

I have known Cora Goldman for more than seven years and have always found her to be of great spiritual ambition and courage. We have had several treasured conversations.

Cora has always handled her personal affairs and finances with integrity and it has been a pleasure to do business with her.

Cordially,

Thomas D. Cooper, VP
Commercial Bank

* * * * *

To Whom it May Concern:

I wanted to let you know that I have had the privilege and opportunity to work with missionary Cora Goldman on several occasions. We partnered with her a couple of years ago to do some outreach with food from her mission in Welch, West Virginia in the Appalachian Mts. I was extremely impressed with her passion and her love for the people. Since then we have sent a couple different waves of teams down to help with other outreach events. These teams have helped in passing out food and even fixing up some homes. A couple weekends ago, she had an outreach at the Armory in Welch, in which we were a part. Over 500 people were ministered to, thousands of pounds of food was given out, the Gospel was preached, lunch was provided, and people were encouraged.

I am writing this letter to let you know how impressed I am with Sister Cora, and her love and passion for the people. It is extremely impressive; she is completely committed to the people of West Virginia, and to taking the Gospel to them. She uses the ministry of love, food, and whatever material things she can get to them to open the door to share Jesus. I would be open to discuss her ministry with you, but I just wanted to let you know how impressed I am with her work in West Virginia. I pray she will continue ministering for years to come. Our church will continue to partner with her. If you have any questions about Sister Cora or her ministry, please don't hesitate to contact me. May God continue to bless her as she reaches people in Welch, and the surrounding communities.

Sincerely,

Pastor Nate Elarton
Senior Pastor
Bedford Christian Community Assembly of God
www.bccag.org

ONE STEP BEFORE HELL
OR
SATAN WANTS ME, GOD HAS ME.

THANK YOU, JESUS

CONTENTS

Forward		xiii
Chapter 1	MY LIFE AS A CHILD	15
Chapter 2	TRAGEDY STRIKES	23
Chapter 3	WHAT CAUSED DARKNESS	27
Chapter 4	WHAT TRANSFORMED WHEN I MET GOD	33
Chapter 5	TURNING POINT	45
Chapter 6	THE MOMENT I MET GOD	49
Chapter 7	TRANSFORMING MIND	53
Chapter 8	DROPPING OFF OLD WAYS	55
Chapter 9	MATURITY	63
Chapter 10	GROWTH	67
Chapter 11	STRUGGLES	73
Chapter 12	MIRACLES OF GOD	75
Chapter 13	SPIRITUAL WARFARE	79
Chapter 14	APPALACHIAN MOUNTAINS	87
Chapter 15	GOD'S PROMISES	93

FORWARD

Proverb 17:17
A friend loveth at all times.

All through this book, I've tried to show how God has used circumstances to teach me in His walk. I now pass on to you what I have learned, with great hopes that you can glean from my experiences and be helped in yours.

Being raised in poverty, I know hunger. Being rejected, I've felt pain. Losing a child by fire, I know grief. Being divorced, I know deceit.

I was born for this time; I'm determined to serve the hurting, the oppressed, and the forgotten. I'm an ordained, licensed, senior pastor and missionary to the Appalachian Mountains. I'm sold out to the one who died for me. I want my life to count for Jesus, the one who died to give me eternal life. I've read the end of the Bible. The time is now. We must make our lives count. Life depends on sold-out Christians. It's only one step before Hell.

Attitude causes latitude, and when the walls fall down and parents are caught under the debris and they are suffocating, gasping for air, trying to dig themselves out, working towards the little light of hope, only to end up falling backwards into a pit, a lion's den, being bit by the sharp teeth of life, it doesn't matter what skills they use. Nothing works. Putting the blame on anyone doesn't solve the deep, deep, damage of the soul and mind.

There are no manuals to deal with the wounds of unknown action through teens, or the reaction of parents who have inherited undeserved, undetected, unknown generational demons. Parenting is not easy, and my role as a parent has been most difficult. Every battle was like quicksand, buried until only my nose was exposed enough for breath. Existence takes the place of life, and you feel like a failure. You can't quit being a parent, and when counseling with qualified professional people can't get to the bottom of the problem, what's left?

The fires of Hell are blazing all around and through the church while she sleeps. The church reminds me of Jesus praying in the garden while the disciples slept.

Wake up, church. People are screaming for help, and who do they have to turn to? People are trapped in bodies that are controlled by demons of alcohol, drugs, sex, rape, pornography, murder, and suicide. These poor souls are in bondage, crying for help, and no one hears.

The church fears what man would say. They have lost their power, ignoring the needs of the dying. Jesus prayed for demoniacs, healed the sick, raised the dead, and told the disciples they could do all that he had done and even more. Jesus is speaking to the church. He is the same today, yesterday, and forever. Greater is He that is in me than he that is in the world.

We are the people of God. We need to stand up and be the church. Let's not worry about what man says. Be concerned about what God says.

Isn't Jesus our teacher? We can do it, because He did it, and told us we can do it.

God's Mission Outreach
110 Main Street
Box 302
Maple Rapids, MI 48853

CHAPTER 1

MY LIFE AS A CHILD

My mother was 15 years old when she got pregnant for me. My father was forced by my mother's dad to go to the justice of peace and marry her. My father was 18 years old at this time. My mother gave birth to me while still a child herself, at age 16. The neighbor lady and Grandma were left to home to help Mother through the birthing, while Granddad and my father went out in a bad snowstorm to find a doctor. They got home empty-handed. Not long after Dad and Granddad left to find a doctor, Mother began hard labor. Her screams caused Grandma to be nervous. The neighbor lady stayed by Mother and coached her. Grandma couldn't stand to see her daughter in pain and left the room crying. Within a short time, Mother's last scream pushed me into this world. I was never weighed, but Mother said I was about 6 pounds, very small. My birth was not recorded for one month.

I believe me coming into the world and my dad being forced to marry my mother caused him to blame me for his entrapment of marriage. My mother once told me that my father rejected and criticized me and my one brother because we were considered the black sheep of the family. My brother always wanted to work in the garage with our dad, but he was never allowed. My brother felt rejected, unloved, pushed aside and useless. My dad would never talk with his son or me. He always joked around with the other children, but we were made to feel unwanted, rejected, and not good enough. I was the oldest. I guess the only time I did anything right was when I babysat my siblings while our parents would go camping, hunting, and so forth, and at the same time that wasn't always done right, either. I guess Mother was correct. Being a black sheep, and being rejected has given me a call on my life to reach those who have lost hope.

Growing up, we lived with my mother's parents on a rented farm. Grandpa was married before and had 6 children with his first wife, cousin to his second wife. His first wife died of a tubular pregnancy with her seventh child. Grandma was married before and had 4 children. She divorced her first husband, and Grandpa and Grandma Serrels were married and had 2 girls, one of whom was my mother. A combination of 11 children was the total of my Grandpa and Grandma's family. When I was only 3 years old, my grandpa used to pick up potatoes for $.50 a day. This was a huge help in trying to feed all their children. They were very poor farmers, but their love was the cement that built a great foundation. Grandpa loved Grandma very much; he always planted a flower garden and picked her roses. Mother said he spoiled Grandma; she was an only child, and didn't have to work. Grandpa pampered her and waited on her hand and foot. Grandma was a good wife. The kitchen would always smell of bread and pies. I never heard a disagreement between Grandpa and Grandma. On the other hand, my parents' marriage always seemed very rocky, constant arguing and fighting. It seemed as if everyone got along in the house, Granddad loved his son-in-law, but the fighting between my parents stirred up frustration. Granddad never involved himself in their fights.

Granddad died when my dad was away in the army. This was in World War II. Granddad didn't feel well, so he went home to rest. After a few hours, Mother went to see if he was okay, and found him dead. I remember all the crying, and my brother and I were rushed off to some relatives. My dad tried to come home for the funeral, but couldn't. I remember the funeral service was held in the front yard of their house.

During this time that our father was away, my brother and I slept with our mother. While Mother would get dressed for bed, she sang the song

> *'Oh she jumped in bed*
> *and covered up her head*
> *and said I could not find her,*
> *but I jumped in behind her.'*

My brother and I would cover our heads so our mother couldn't find us. Then we all snuggled and went to sleep. There is very little that I remember about my childhood, but when my mother sang that song to me, I can always recall such a good time. She was a good more, and for that I am grateful.

I was just a little over 3 years old when Daddy came home from the war. It was at night, and Mother's baby sister and her husband drove in the yard. Sometimes, Mother seemed to know things without anyone telling her. I don't know how, but she ran out to the car and opened the back door and my dad was lying on the floor, covered up with his coat. Instead of Dad surprising her, she surprised him. They call came in the house and there was such happiness. Mother was lifted from her feet and Daddy held her in his arms as he kissed her. I don't recall him paying any attention to me, but he picked up my brother John and kissed him. I stood back a little ways. I remember looking up at this tall soldier in his uniform, and even then the years of rejection from my father were evident by his attitude and actions towards me. It was my father who, from the time I was a child, gave me the patriotic red, white and blue heart. I love America.

My mother told me that Dad went to war as a young man, and came home an old one. My daddy was on the front line. He talked very little about his war-time experiences. But I believe he re-lived daily all the killing, and drinking became what he did to suppress his feelings. Fighting with my mother was a common thing when he drank. Being the oldest child, it was my job to take the guns away from Daddy when he was drunk.

My eyes lit up to see my father in his uniform, this soldier so tall, and remembering Mother sitting at her desk, writing letters from home, and crying. Now he was home. I was about in 5th grade when I learned what World War II had accomplished to keep America free, and in my mind I pictured this man in uniform, so I looked up to him. He then became my hero. As far as the rejection I felt from him,

I learned to accept that. Rejection was common in my life; I learned to live with it. I can't change people; I can change my attitude and hold no grudges.

After Granddad's death, things changed. Mom and Dad moved from Grandma's house. I'm not sure why we had to move. When we found a house, Grandma moved in with us. We didn't have many beds, and Grandma and I slept together. Sometimes we moved up to three times a year. I hated moving. I believe Dad had many flashbacks from the war and that is why he was unable to hold down a job. I presume Dad's mind was messed up with the scars from the war.

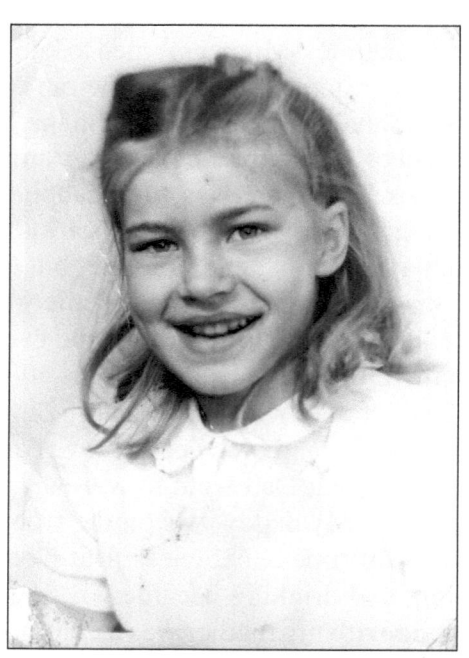

CORA AT 8 YEARS OLD

I remember when I was in kindergarten. We moved into a house so decrepit, you could stand outside and look through the holes in the walls and see the people inside. There were times when I would wake up during the night and have snow on the bed. My mother had it real hard, living in that house. Even in the winter, she would have to take my brother and me in a wagon to the neighbors to get water. There was no plumbing of any kind in the house. Mother did dishes in dishpans and had a wood stove to cook on. I recall an old wooden table and four chairs. I can't remember any cupboards in the kitchen. I don't know where Mother got her couch, but it was so uncomfortable, with the springs coming through and pieces of stuffing missing, so it showed the wood. Mother tried to keep the couch covered at all times. She did without a lot, but I never heard her complain.

We moved in with my aunt just a few miles from where I was born in Blanchard, MI. It was called the mandabrants. My brother, John, Mom and Dad lived in this house. I remember Mother going back in the woods to get wood for heat. She was pregnant and lost that baby. Mother was a great woman.

That year, I got a doll for Christmas. I think my aunt bought it. When I was a second-grader, my brother and I had to walk more than a mile to school. That year, I had pencils and paper along with crayons at school, but when my parents moved on a weekend, I wasn't able to go get my stuff from school. I was really hurt. I never had much to call my own, and now this was gone, in the move from a country school to a town school.

I loved my maternal Grandma Serrels. I remember her living with my aunt on the farm. She was the best. Grandma was a diabetic, but she ate what she shouldn't have. She later died in her sleep, and after that my aunt said she had seen her rocking in her chair. What my aunt had seen was the ghost of Grandma. It wasn't at all scary to talk about her conversation with the dead; it all seemed natural.

I believe this was my first experience into the world of psychic phenomena. To think that Grandma loved her family enough to make a visit after her passing comforted us. Looking back, I know it wasn't a ghost, it was a demon disguised as Grandma. After that, my aunt really got into the Ouija board. She would talk to what she thought were dead loved ones, possibly for the thrill of hearing from those she missed. Mother used Tarot cards. It was fun to have your fortune told, and Mother was real good.

On my father's side, his uncles and family members would have séances. Several would sit around the oak table, and that table danced so hard that its legs broke off. This demonic activity was very strong. I don't even know if those people were aware of the power they were working with. What starts out being a game when you are in control later turns to the control of the demons. This event was in the earlier years of my dad's uncle's life. I don't even know if my dad was born at this time. Mother told me the story so I would know this was a generational thing, and it was okay to seek the spiritual world.

KIRBY FAMILY MEMBERS WHO WERE INVOLVED IN THE SÉANCE THAT MADE THE OAK TABLE DANCE

Dad got a job as a mechanic at Caswels garage in Six Lakes, Michigan. Everyone said he was real good, and reasonable. Things started to look better for our family. But that year, I came down with scarlet fever, and I had to stay quarantined in a dark room. I was out of school for about three weeks. When I went back, my marks had dropped from A's and B's to D's and E's. Part of this was because I had bad eyes, and didn't get glasses until I was in my teens. School now seemed to be very hard for me.

Then my father lost his job as a mechanic because there was not enough work. My father had to move in with my mother's sister and her family. My dad was looking for work in Elsie, Michigan through all this, leaving my mother at home with four children and no money to feed them. We used to go out in the fields and turn over cow pies to get the grubs, catch crickets and dig worms. We sold the bait to put food on the table.

We finally moved not far from my aunt's house when I was 11 years old. It was the nicest house we ever lived in, until one night. While we were all sleeping, the house caught fire because of faulty electrical wiring. It burned to the ground, and we lost everything. Dad was able to buy a house through a friend who loaned him the money. I had my 12th birthday in Bannister.

Everything I ever wore was hand-me-downs. My mother never bought any clothing or shoes. The only shoes I had were dancing shoes with open heel and toe. I was teased on the playground every day. One day, I had one friend and she turned everyone else against me. The next day, she was their friend and I was alone. Rejection should have been my name. That year, for my birthday, some of the kids came knocking on my door, and put a box in my hand and ran off. It was a brand new pair of shoes. It was the nicest thing anyone had ever done for me before. I always thought that it never made sense that I was made fun of and rejected, and then given a pair of shoes. I don't know if the holiday spirit got into the girls, but one girl's parents worked at the variety store, and from there these shoes were purchased, with all the girls putting in for them. It wasn't any different going back to school, but I was still rejected, but my feet were warm. I know what it feels like to be rejected, and I like building on those who have lost hope, and through love I have been able to reach into the lives and see lives change for the best.

I ended up quitting high school to get a job in a restaurant, and also did babysitting. The owner's son asked me out to a New Year's Eve party, and he was supposed to take me home afterwards. I ended up getting drunk and I passed out on the couch. When I came to, I was being raped; all I could do was cry. I knew right then that I was pregnant. I went home to my parent's house. I was scared to death. I was 17 and I had no answers to life.

Then one of the town boys, Bill, began to talk to me and came to my home to date me, but I said no! He came back later and said God told him I was pregnant and he loved me, and he wanted to marry me. We dated, and a month later we were married. Bill and I ended up buying his parent's 40-acre farm and started our family.

CHAPTER 2

TRAGEDY STRIKES

My oldest son, Darrell idolized his little brother, Barry Lynn. They were great buddies. Bill worked nights and I was left home alone with the children. I remember one night hearing a noise outside, and when I looked out the window, I saw a lit cigarette going through the orchard. Every time I called the police, they never found any evidence of anyone there.

DARRELL AND BARRY LYNN

SATAN WANTS ME, GOD HAS ME.

At Halloween, I had been invited to go shopping with friends, Darrell was 5, Barry Lynn was 3 ½, and I left the children with a baby sitter. Bill had been tearing the siding off the house and was burning it. The neighbors had called and ask Bill to help in the harvesting of the beans. When Bill left to go help, he told me to check the fire before leaving. I did and it was only smoldering, so I thought it looked pretty safe.

I was told we had been gone about 15 minutes when Darrell and Barry Lynn got hold of some empty cans and played with them. Someone had broken the lock on our storage tank for gas for the tractor. The boys filled the cans with gas. I'm not sure why they would do something like this; my only guess is that they may have seen gas thrown on logs before and saw what it could do, not knowing the dangers that lay ahead. While running with the cans, some gas spilled on Barry Lynn. When the gas went into the smoldering remains of the fire and came back out, he ignited.

The husband of one of my friends found us shopping. He grabbed my arm and told me one of the boys had been burned. There was a police escort waiting outside to lead us to the hospital.

When I got to the hospital, Barry Lynn was in the emergency room, crying for his mama. They wouldn't let me go to him. Barry was in the elevator going up for emergency surgery. He said his shoe hurt his foot, but he didn't have shoes on. During surgery, they put a tube up his leg. He said he couldn't see, but his eyes were closed. I was told not to talk to him. I didn't, but I have always wished I had. I was told I couldn't stay at the hospital with Barry Lynn, but after what happened that day, I swore no one would ever again keep me from my children when they needed me.

Mother took the boys home with her. Everyone told me Barry Lynn was going to be okay, and I believed that. That night, when I was fast asleep, I was awakened by a voice coming from my closet that said, "Come with me, come with me." I looked at the clock, and thought the sound was just Bill watching TV. I went back to sleep. When the phone rang at 2:30 A.M., it was someone from the hospital saying to hurry and get there, because Lynn had taken a turn for the worst.

The main road was all torn up, and we had to take detours. By the time we got to the hospital, it was too late. The doctor met us outside and said he was sorry, Barry Lynn had expired. I had never heard that word before, but I knew what it meant. I fell to the ground from the weight of the pain and shock. The doctor asked if I wanted to see my son, and of course I said yes. We were taken to a room where a sheet was pulled over this tiny body. The doctor pulled the sheet back, and I saw a perfect, unscarred body. No burns, yet despite what I saw in the hospital, there was a closed casket at the funeral. Later, I was told that my mother was holding Barry Lynn on the ride to the hospital, and when he scratched his face, flesh fell off in his hands. I believe God knew I wouldn't have been able to handle the sight, and He protected me for that time and the future. Only God knows how much we can take, even when we are not His child.

As I write this, I'm having flashbacks and crying hard. I loved my son, and even though I wasn't a Christian then, I now look forward to seeing my son in Heaven, along with mother and grandparents.

After Barry Lynn's death, I blamed myself, saying I must have been a bad mother. I was put in the hospital with a nervous breakdown. I was on Valium for a year-and-a-half. I don't even remember taking care of my family. Even though I didn't know God, He knew me. He was with me. What Satan means for bad, God can turn around for good. Barry Lynn's' death started me on a search in my life. I can relate to those who have lost children, and I know all things do work out for good. I started going to church after the funeral.

I searched for answers to the voice I heard, and to the meaning behind it. What caused it? Why had I heard it? Pastors told me I was crazy, that I didn't hear what I said I heard. My friend Dolores was a Catholic, and she set up a meeting with her priest. He took me through the church and showed me statues and told me stories of people who had seen these visions of people. He told me he believed the voice saying, "Come to me, come to me," had two meaning. One, that God was calling me to the hospital, and the other, that God was calling me to Himself. The priest said he would go to the hospital to find out what time Barry Lynn had taken his turn for the worst. He found out it was exactly at 1:30, when I was awakened by the voice.

It wasn't long after Barry Lynn's death that strange things began to manifest in our house. There were unfamiliar voices, sometimes it sounded like several voices, and mingled so it was hard to understand what the voices were saying. We would hear footsteps going up and down the stairs. We had a light on the wall at the top of the stairs with a broken chain. The only way to turn the light off was to unscrew the bulb. I used to unscrew the bulb until it was only hanging by a thread, and by the time I reached the bottom of the stairs, the light would go on. When I went to check, the bulb was now screwed in tight. Toys that were under the bed would be pulled out as though they were being played with.

One time I was at home alone, forgetting my children were at my mothers' house. There were some jars sitting on the steps to go upstairs, and I heard them knocking together as though they would break. But no one was visible. We had gone to a wedding and left my cousin to take care of the boys, and when we got home, he was as white as a sheet. He said the toy piano began to play, but no one was around. He was scared to death. He quickly left the house, vowing, "I will never come in this house again." He kept that promise. My sister-in-law was living with us while my brother was in the army. Once when she was sitting on the bed upstairs, the door flew open and a cat flew in the door to her bedroom as though someone had thrown it. My sister-in-law moved out and never came back.

All of these occurrences opened the door to occult experiences for me, which led deeper into mysticism. One day, while I was sitting in the little church I attended at that time, the pastor used some big words I didn't know the meaning of, and all of a sudden his preaching was drowned out by a voice telling me I was going to be a pastor. At the time that I heard the voice saying I was going to be a pastor, I believed it was God preparing me for the future, knowing the route that I was going to take, and the downhill spiral I would experience, so I could relate to those in the occult. God never left me. Even though I never knew Him then, He carried me through.

CHAPTER 3

WHAT CAUSED DARKNESS

I went to cosmetology school and graduated in 1966, at the same time I was a full-time mother to three children: Darrell, Wendell, and Tamara. After I graduated. I got a job in a beauty shop a few miles away from my home in Ashley, Michigan. One day, the owner went shopping and left me in charge of the customers. I had all my customers under the dryers, and in walked a woman who told me she was two weeks early to get her hair cut, but God had sent her. My antennas went up. I had been searching for answers. The churches all said I was crazy. Now God sent this woman to talk to me.

She began telling me things about my dead son, and for the first time I was getting answers. How could anyone know things about me or Barry Lynn unless it was from God? She invited me to her spiritualist church, saying she was sure I would be able to talk to Barry Lynn. I told her I would go if my mother would go. When I went home and told mother about the church services, and she agreed to go. She said all churches were the same, but I know now she was wrong.

This spiritualist church met in the basement of a two-story, old-fashioned church in the country, in a town called Sigles. I knew no one in the room, except this person who had come to the beauty shop. A total stranger stood before me and said my son and grandmother were there. I received messages from Barry and my beloved Grandma Serrels. Then things seemed to go a little crazy for me.

Supposedly, Grandma told a story of my watering the chickens at the age of three. My mother told me not to, because I would get the wood wet. Mother gave me a spanking for disobeying, and Grandma gave me a cookie when I cried. When we left the church, I told Mother we weren't going back to that kind of nonsense. No such thing ever happened, with the chickens and the water, the wood pile and spanking and cookie.

Mother surprised me by saying everything in that story was true. It all happened, just as I was told. Well, this made a big difference. We continued to go to that church, and then met in the home of the customer from the beauty shop. The more we met, the more messages I would get from the spirit world and passed on to those in the group. I never knew who these messages were for, but once I spoke what I was given, the individual the message applied to would speak up. One time I remember giving a message about someone's basement, and describing a World War II soldier who was in the basement of the house. I learned I had touched on the life of the soldier's great-grandchild who was having great difficulties and wondering why strange things were happening in her basement. Now everything was clear, and the mystery of the activities was solved.

I so wanted to be able to help people, and I believed all I was doing was just that. Helping. I didn't know I was serving the 'little g' god. I thought I was serving the 'Big G' God. I didn't know there was a devil, and I knew very little about the 'big G' God. I thought I had a gift, and I was going to do my best to help anyone I could.

One night after one of the meetings, I went home and as usual when I got into bed that night, I pulled the covers over my head and then pulled them back down to uncover my head. When I did, at the foot of my bed I saw a huge owl, about three feet high. I again covered my head, this time in fear. I didn't understand the meaning, and when I got brave and uncovered my head, the owl was gone. I tried without success to get the owl to appear and it would not. When I went to another meeting and told this story to the medium I was learning under, she said this was my guide, Great Owl, and if I ever needed him, all I had to do was to call him.

Great Owl was an Indian chief. I was later given two more guides, Sister Teresa, a nun, and Doctor Tom, a Black man. My guide now directed me in psychometrics. This involved using a personal article belonging to the deceased, such as jewelry. I would take the article and place it on my forehead, and it was like watching color television. I received from the past and present. I was helping people get through their struggles over a death, and I felt like this was what I was born to do. I felt good about helping.

I never put curses on people; I only tried to help people. I tried to bridge the gap between the living and the dead. What I was doing is called witchcraft, but I didn't know that. One hears of black witchcraft and white witchcraft. If someone had asked me at that time, I would have called what I was doing white. But in the world, this is all witchcraft, and neither one is right. God is a jealous God, and He wants no other gods before Him.

There were many times that I would give readings and the so-called dead would speak through me to their loved ones. I was very successful in my readings. It took three mediums to verify the legitimacy of my readings, for me to become ordained within the spiritualist church. The people within the church were all elderly and I was the youngest of the mediums there, and these women were determined that I would take over the pulpit. Now if I had been given this opportunity in the beginning of my learning, I believed I would have said yes. Now that the opportunity came, I said no, and I refused to be ordained.

Then someone reminded me about the voice I heard in church once, that told me I was going to be a pastor. I still would not bring myself to say yes to the pulpit.

When I first got started in the spiritualist meetings, Darrell, my oldest, was very sick. I didn't have money to take him to the doctor, so I took him to a meeting and the people prayed for him. He started upchucking, and he was made well. Consider this, however: John 10:10 says the thief comes to steal and kill, so if Satan can put sickness on a body, he can remove it. Every time something like this happened, I got stronger and stronger and more deeply into Satan's work, because I saw results. Not everything Satan does is all lies. He mixes truth with error, and the cults and involvement with the occult are growing by leaps and bounds. However, at that time, I still thought God was the one performing all these wonderful miracles.

I innocently played a game that began to control me like a magnet. I would be drawn to the Ouija board. The board told me many things. One time when we were playing it, the board told me I was pregnant and I was going to have a little girl. I said that was a lie, but you know what? It was true. I was pregnant, and I did have a little girl.

While I was working at the beauty shop one day during this time, I got a call that my house was on fire. By the time I got home, everything was gone, there was nothing left. We were told by inspectors that the dryer caused the fire. But the dryer was not on. Then we were told it was electrical, and someone else said we were smoking in bed, but neither of us smoked. At the time of the fire, Bill's folks both worked in Lansing and staying at her mother's house, so we were able to move into their house. The first night there, we got a call that our barn had burned to the ground. When we got over to the farm, we learned that the wind blew sparks from the apple tree to the barn and sat the straw on fire. The apple tree was close to the house, and without anyone knowing, the fire from the house caught the inside of the rotted tree on fire. The wind picked up at night and sparks were seen by neighbors ascending in the direction of the barn. Our house and contents were insured for $1,500, the barn was insured for $2,000, so all we had to start out with after the fire was $3,500. We made something out of nothing; the fires did not stop us from moving on. Even though we were not Christians, I believe God watched over us.

After living a while at my in-laws' house, we had a few people over for a séance. This was my first attempt at contacting the dead. I made the older children go upstairs to bed before we started. When they started screaming, I went upstairs to check on them, and saw cards among other things being thrown around. My six-month-old niece was on the day bed and had been picked up and thrown on the floor. So I had the children come downstairs in my bedroom. When all this activity was taking place, I didn't understand the connection to séances. I thought this stuff was all of God in Heaven. I was very naïve and innocent. I didn't have anyone to teach me right from wrong. This is why I write my experiences now, to try to help those who are also blinded, just as I was. After putting the children to bed,

I went into the kitchen where everyone was waiting, and the door slammed so hard behind me that I screamed.

There were about 13 of us at the table. When I got started, I prayed for God to come to us, protect us and bring our loved ones to talk to us. I didn't know I was talking to the 'little g' god, Satan. I thought I was talking to the God of Heaven, who I didn't know. Spiritually, I heard a car door slam and I heard voices. Without warning, spirits took over my body. My hands twisted into the shape of a crippled claw. The séance was stopped and my mother ran cold water over my hands until they went back to normal.

Well, I knew I had done something wrong, so I went to the medium I studied under to get help. We tried another séance in the home of my teacher in the little town of North Starr. This time, there were 16 people sitting around the table. We all held hands, and I sat at the head of the table. I prayed just as I did the week before at my in-laws' house. All the lights were off, but the mercury lights from outside lit up the room we were in. The third person to the right of me said, "Look at her. Her hair is pulled back. She looks like my sister-in-law that died two weeks ago." In the corner in back of me was a straight back chair, and it started dancing. The woman who was teaching me said it was Red Horse, an Indian chief who was my mother's guide. The dishes in the china cabinet were dancing so hard, we thought they were going to break.

Then I began experiencing a hard time of breathing. I felt like I was being choked. It was awful. Those around me prayed over me, and after several hours, I was able to breath with no problem. Remember John 10:10: the thief comes to steal, kill and destroy, but God comes to give life. As Satan tries to kill, he can reverse the damage that he does. I also believe in that last part, that says 'but God gives life.'

God knew the forthcoming events, and even though I wasn't a Christian, I believe God protected me and my angels took care of me. I truly believe that whatever happens in our lives, God is in it, and with faith, all bad can be turned to good to help others who might be going through what we have already been through.

That night as we left the séance, I was in a weakened condition. I was drained and could hardly talk. Mother was driving her truck, and all I could remember was seeing trees and a ditch. Years later, I asked her what that was all about. She said while she was driving, Satan tried to take her steering away and she fought to keep control. She took her foot off the gas pedal, but the pedal went to the floor. As we were rushing towards the ditch, my mother and my sister said the Lord's Prayer, and then Mother was once again in control. God was watching out for us all back then, even though we didn't belong to Him.

CHAPTER 4

WHAT TRANSFORMED WHEN I MET GOD

The following week was extraordinary. A lady in our hometown had a serious accident and the Rainbow Lake Board Association asked me to take up a donation to help the family out. It's really remarkable how God works things out. I stopped at one house, and the woman there said she had heard about the accident, gave a donation, and then invited me to a new, developing church. I said okay.

My reasoning was, "I'm going 20 miles to the church I attend. Mother said all churches are going to Heaven, and it is only three miles to your church, so I'll see you Sunday." I followed through with my promise, and I went to church.

Let me tell you, my mother was wrong and all churches are not going to Heaven. For the first time, I heard hellfire and brimstone in a sermon.

The pastor was preaching on the rich man and the poor man in Luke 16, the only time in all my years that I heard that message from the pulpit. I really believe God had the stage set for me; this was my day. This is Jesus' parable where the rich man asked Father Abraham to send someone to tell his brothers there really was a Hell. Father Abraham's reply was, "They have Moses and the prophets. Let your brothers hear them." The rich man said, "No, Father Abraham, if they hear from the dead they will believe." Father Abraham said, "No one can go speak to them from either side."

I knew then, those who were speaking through me and the séances, Ouija board, and tarot cards, were all of Satan. It was not loved ones speaking from the realm of the dead, but demons disguised as loved ones.

Oh, God, I have taken so many people to those séances. I thought this was all from You. Oh, God, bring those people back into my life so I can tell them the truth.

I knew then, in 1971, that I was going to Hell. The pastor kept talking and I kept sliding down in my chair. In my mind, I kept saying, "I'm going to Hell, I don't want to go to Hell."

I accepted Jesus Christ as my Savior, and let me tell you, 50 pounds dropped from my left side. I felt it go. All the occult powers I had were gone. When I accepted Jesus as my personal savior, I felt emptied of a weight that had controlled me, my mind was clear, I felt new. My body was light and I felt like I could fly. I was free. I had peace and joy fill my soul. What was dark now became light. I had never heard the gospel of Jesus dying for me to save me from my sins. I didn't know what I was missing until this day. The life I lived was so natural, just like breathing, and now I had a new excitement fill me. I wanted to tell everyone I met about my new relationship with Jesus.

Look at Saul. He thought he was serving the living God by killing multitudes of Christians. I thought I was serving God by giving readings to those who came into my life. Oh, God, forgive me. I repent.

Then there was Mary Magdalene, who had seven demons until Jesus met her. When she was delivered, she faithfully followed Jesus. I had three demon guides that I would call on to get things done. For instance, once I was waiting for some relatives and we were half an hour late for the meeting at the spiritualist church, so I called on my guides to not let the meeting start until we got there. Just as soon as we sat down, the meeting started. That night they had an artist there who drew pictures of dead loved ones who were there among the people attending the meeting. I told my guides I wanted a picture of someone who was by me. There was three pictures drawn and given out, and I received one. I was told this was a great aunt.

Mother knew her. We went to her cousin and she got a picture of the aunt and showed it to us, and it looked like the picture I had.

Well let me tell you, when I was saved, I burned that picture that was once boldly displayed in my living room, along with all the books, manuals everything that involved spiritualism. It was all burned. For five years, I had served Satan, and thought I was serving God in Heaven.

After I got out of the spiritualist church, I heard of black and white witchcraft. As I said before, what I had been doing, I would have called white. Some say white witchcraft is okay. I never put curses on people. I never killed people, as black witchcraft does. I only tried to help people. But let me tell you, both are wrong in the eyes of God. Had I died in my sin, I would have gone to Hell.

I can remember, at the very end of my involvement in the spiritualist church, I had tried to read the Bible, but I couldn't understand anything I read. I cried, because I wanted to understand, so I took the Bible to the woman that had mentored me in spiritualism, to get her help. She told me she only knew of two verses in the Bible, and one was the instruction that if someone was sick, to give them a hanky or apron that would be prayed over, and people would be healed. She told me to stay away from those Baptist people, because they believed in hellfire, brimstone and fear.

But God ultimately set me on the steps of a Baptist pastor. I ended up in the Baptist church. Praise God.

When I was giving readings, I never charged for them because I loved helping people, and I had people coming from all over. I don't even know how they found out about me. One lady many miles away from me called and asked if I would read for her. Others had tried to read for her without success. When she came to my house, I took a piece of jewelry, put it to my head, and saw so many crazy things, I told her I didn't want to read. She begged me, so I finally told her what I had gotten.

"There's a man with a gun holding up a pharmacy. I see him in jail behind bars, dressed like a clown."

She said, "That's my husband. He robbed a pharmacy, he's in jail, and he's always clowning around."

Well that opened the doors, and periodically she would come to my home for a reading. After my salvation, she called and wanted a reading, and I told her everything we had been doing was of the devil, and I didn't do that anymore. I witnessed salvation to her, and she said, "I'm so glad for you. I'll come up and see you sometime."

That was over 30 years ago, but I have never seen the woman again. My life was totally changed. Before salvation, Satan was my father and he knew my thoughts. After salvation, God became my father, and the only way Satan knows what is going to happen is for him to hear me speak it.

As a parent and mother, I was not perfect. I've made my mistakes. Every time I saw a baby, I wanted one of my own. I loved my babies the best I knew how. In their infant stages, I could cuddle and kiss them, and they returned that love to me. I was father, mother, and disciplinarian. Before Bill and I married, we visited with family and friends. This was wonderful. One week after we were married, we picked my mother up to go visit friends who didn't go to the wedding. After we dropped Mother off at home and we were on our way home, Bill told me to never ask him to go visit anyone again. He didn't like doing that, but if I wanted to, I could. That was the way it was for the rest of our 39-year marriage. Bill didn't participate with the family.

I didn't have money to take the children anywhere, but I tried to make memories. I always thought we would be a close-knit family. We would go to the woods to pick berries, apples and nuts. This was fun. Later, I got a babysitting job and would take the children for a hamburger or ice cream cone. I did my best, but I have failed in many ways Sometimes your best just isn't good enough, when children are suffering and you don't know it.

As the children got older, their problems grew. It was becoming very hard to deal with Darrell. He was very hard on me. He drained me mentally and physically. He would take the whole world on without a second thought. His rebellion toward authority grew stronger every day. He didn't want to obey rules. He thought he could run his own life, and at 13, curfews were not for him. He thought he could come and go as he pleased and tell me what to do. I was determined not to let him destroy his life. I didn't know much about being a mother to a rebellious teenager, but I knew these children were not mine, they were only loaned to me, and I only had one shot to do my best.

I remember seeing spoiled children treating their parents with disrespect, sassing and just plain mean. I said if I had children like that, I would raise them like I was raised, with correction, using a belt and groundings. Darrell was worse than any parent's nightmare. I did everything the way I was taught, and nothing worked. Darrell was a rebel. Correction didn't work, love made no difference, and grounding only forced him to sneak out at night. At 13 years old, he was brought home by the police for drinking. He never told on those who were responsible for getting him the booze. He even took the blame for what others did. I prayed, cried, and was at my wit's end, trying to get through, and with no result. Darrell wanted the world, and I fought for this child's soul that Satan wanted.

I knew Darrell blamed himself for his brother's death. Five years after Barry's passing, Mother told me that when she had brought Darrell back after the funeral that I had blamed him. I know this must have set in like cement and his reaction to life became hard. For three years, I don't remember taking care of my family. I had had a nervous breakdown. I was hospitalized and took Valium like candy. Sometimes I would take more than prescribed. I was like a zombie. I was numb. I can relate to those who do drugs and act crazy and don't know what they have done. I have been given such a compassion for teens hurting like Darrell hurt, for alcoholics, druggies who are caught up in life's web and don't know how to get out. I write this for those who are struggling with similar situations, to tell them there is hope if only we can realize all things work together for good for those called of God. Darrell, like many, had a battle raging inside. Their only communication is to do what Darrell had done. They are locked up in a prison, and their only escape is rebellion, acting out, and make someone recognize their cries, and help.

Darrell watched his brother burn up. My mother told me that I blamed Darrell for being the oldest and not protecting his little brother, and I am sure this caused Darrell's troubles. At eight years old, he began to withdraw from people. He became a loner. I believe Darrell wanted to be punished for his brother's death. When he did something wrong, when he was in places he shouldn't have been, he left all of his information, and the law always came to our home after B&Es, or whatever the crime. Darrell was in his own prison of guilt, and I am sure he had flashbacks as well. I couldn't help this dear child. I didn't understand, yet I knew he blamed himself for his brother's death and no one would listen. I tried to tell his councilors that he was blaming himself and he wanted to be punished, but I was just the mother, they thought I didn't know anything and no one wanted to hear me.

Darrell was a kind-hearted child. He would risk his life to save another. Like the time the boat tipped and he helped his friend to shore, or the time I took the children in the woods to pick blackberries and Tamara, who was four years old at the time, stepped into a nest of yellow jackets. Darrell ran to her rescue and was all stung up.

At 13, Darrell was put in a foster home. It was reported to the police that Darrell, along with friends, had broken into a home and stole a car. They were traveling 90 miles an hour on a dirt road and lost control and hit a tree. The ensuing investigation ended up in court. Darrell became a ward of the court and was placed in a foster home.

Darrell had been in the foster home about three months. I had been saved about two years and was still experiencing a new life. I know if God had not been in my life, I might not have made it through this difficult time. One night, I had done the laundry and was taking clothes to the bedroom and the Holy Spirit hit me hard. I fell to my knees at my bed. I looked at the clock and saw it was 11:30. When I went to my knees, I had no sense of anything unusual happening. It was like being boxed in and the Holy Spirit had total control. I yelled and felt totally drained. For the first time, I didn't ask God to protect Darrell with no harm. I said, "God, do whatever it takes to get Darrell saved, even if it means his death. I want him to go Heaven."

When I finished praying, I dropped in bed, worn out. At 1 a.m., I received a call from the hospital that Darrell had taken all the medicines in his foster parents' house. His stomach was pumped and Darrell didn't die. His foster parents didn't want him back, so he came back home to my house. Darrell was accepted back home with arms wide open. Everything was put in the past, and I believed he would learn from his experiences and we were now on the road to recovery.

At 17, Darrell wanted to go into the service and Bill signed for him. What a relief, I thought, someone is going to help him get his life on track. I couldn't. I prayed, thanking God that Darrell was going to finally get a good start on life. He went for a physical and the x-ray machine broke down with the person just ahead of him, so they passed Darrell through. Later, we found that Darrell had a curved spine and he would never have passed. Through prayer, God took care of Darrell. My prayers were heard and answered. Darrell loved boot camp and the time he spent in the army.

DARRELL AT 17, ARMY PHOTO

The following weekend, Darrell went to church with us and listened to a speaker from Teen Challenge. Everyone had their heads bowed, and from the back I heard someone walking up to the altar.

I kept saying, "God, let it be Darrell," and when I opened my eyes, it was Darrell. He went to the assistant pastor and told him when he asked Jesus in his heart he felt warm all over. The pastor said, "You don't feel anything." Let me tell you, God can do anything, any way He wants to. Well, this remark took away the excitement of salvation, and for 32 years, Darrell was like a fish out of water.

Bill used to beat Darrell; he would get him on the floor and kick him. How many times I had to pull Bill off. How I cried. I know Bill blamed Darrell for Barry's death, and Darrell didn't feel loved. This is so hard to write, but I must, because I know there will be those who read this whose lives have been woven into a shambles, and you feel there is no way out. All I can say is, there is hope. Don't give up, God loves you.

When Darrell was 15, he was put in a boys' juvenile home. He called home, asking for personal hygiene things, including razor blades. I got all these things and took them to him. When I got home, I went to my prayer closet, in my bedroom, and looked up to the ceiling and just thanked God for how Darrell was doing. I had a long, drawn-out talk with God and it was great.

I felt great until the next day, when I received a call from Darrell's unit. Darrell had gone into the showers, and when he didn't come out for a long time, those in authority went in to look for him. They found Darrell with both wrists slit with the razor blades I had taken to him. He had written a suicide note, saying he was to blame for his brother's death. Darrell survived the suicide attempt and another trust issue of letting God be God. Darrell was in the hospital just a couple days, and I know God heard and answered the prayers of his mother. This was a true eye-opener to Darrell's emotional needs, and now people listened and helped him through. Remember when I was getting counseling for him, and told the counselors I believed he blamed himself for his brother's death, and they disagreed? Mothers aren't far off base, despite what many educated psychologists and counselors may think. We live with our children; we know them better than any educated councilor.

After I heard about what Darrell had done, I was very upset with God. I went back into my bedroom and shook my fist in the face of God and told Him I wasn't going to serve Him anymore. He let

Darrell do what he did when things were going so well. I went to walk away, and God spoke to me. He said, "When you speak aloud, Satan hears you. When you were so happy about your son's condition, Satan took the positive and turned it around to negative. Before praying aloud, you tell Satan and his demons they have no power there. You have the authority to close the ears, eyes and mouths of Satan and his demons, then call on the angels of God to get Satan and his demons so far away that they cannot see, hear, or speak." This made sense.

Through tears, I apologized to God and asked for forgiveness. It was like a light bulb going on inside me. I knew God had used this experience to change my prayer life. I was being taught the power of my tongue. When Satan was my father, he knew my thoughts. Now he only hears me speak, and turns my words around for destruction. I believe this is where God says 'Greater is He that is in you than he that is in the world.' As Christians, we can make Satan and his demons leave from around us before prayer. We have the power through God.

Darrell grew up spiritually through this suicide attempt. People seemed to understand better what he was going through. He was blaming himself for Barry Lynn's death, and now it was all in the open and he could deal with life. When I prayed for Darrell, I would close the ears, eyes, and mouth of Satan and his demons and ask the angels of God to get them so far away they could not see, hear or speak. Then I applied Ephesians 5:20, I Thessalonians 5:18. "In everything give thanks, for this is the will of the Lord concerning you." So what I go through in my life and what you go through in your life is God's will, bad or good. So no matter what I go through in life, thanking God in it, the Lord will see me through it. So God, I thank You in the fact that Darrell attempted suicide, but you changed that. Thank You in the fact that Darrell has been blaming himself for Barry's death. Thank You in the fact that Darrell doesn't feel loved, but God, You change that. Darrell was now on the road to recovery. Thank God.

I believe being a parent is one of the hardest jobs in life. To know what to do and when to do it and how. None of my babies came with instructions. I didn't get a book to tell me how. I remember the first pastor I had. He said the most beautiful thing in the world is a newborn baby, but it's like a lit piece of dynamite and it can go off any time.

I may not have been the best mother, but I did the best that I could. Those who struggle with a wounded child and you've done your best, it's time to turn it all over to God. God knew from the time of conception what each one of us would go through in our lives. Nothing surprises Him. Thanking God in all I have gone through has helped me to accept things I can't change, change things I can, and try to help others going through similar situations. Knowing that all things work together for those who love the Lord, called for His purpose, remember you are not alone. It is for His purpose, not ours.

I was on my way home one day, and God said to go over and see a relative. I said no! I tried to visit before and was kicked out of their house. My two daughters were molested by their sons, and I called the police to report it. Reporting to the police this event of molestation put my family members in an uproar. There was strain in relationships. There was never any conviction, but I believe the event could have prevented future molestations from happening. If I had to do it all over again, I would have done the same thing. At the time God told me to go to that house, it had been five years since I had seen them. God said, "You send the Holy Spirit ahead, close the ears, eyes and mouth of Satan and his demons. Send the angels ahead to get the devil and demons so far away that they cannot see, hear or speak." I did, and God did, and the doors were open. As I was doing what God said to do, I felt fear come up in me, but boldness took over and I was boxed in with power from on high. I had peace, but I never stopped praying and praising God. When I went to the house and knocked on the door, I was met with a spirit of dislike, but the Holy Spirit lived through to new relationships, and slowly I made my way back for visits. It works, so I use this principle a lot.

I was witnessing to a young man, and when I ask him if he was saved, he said he was. God spoke to me and said he was not. In my mind, I said, "God, send your angels to close the ears, eyes and mouth of Satan and his demons, so they cannot hear, see or speak." You see, before we are saved, Satan is our father, and the spirit within the unsaved will not let the material man understand.

So after letting the angels do their work, I asked this young man, "If you were to die, where would you go? Heaven or Hell?"

He said, "I would probably go to Hell."

I said, "Do you want to?"

He said no. He accepted Christ Jesus as Savior and I directed him to a gospel preaching church. God's word says if we have the faith the size of a mustard seed, we can move mighty mountains. It's planting time.

Sometimes we make work out of whatever we do. It's time to let go and let God. The Holy Spirit is speaking, so be quiet, listen and follow.

CHAPTER 5

TURNING POINT

When Satan was my father, I served him, believing the powers I had were all from God in Heaven. I was fooled (Matthew 6:24). The Bible says we cannot serve two masters. We will hate one and love the other. There are many people who are fooled just as I was. They do not understand the dangers of the world's master that they serve. One sees the power and thinks it comes from God in Heaven, never realizing it comes from the 'little g' god, Satan.

When I changed masters in my life and my life was renewed through the Holy Spirit, my spirit walk and thinking did transform. I no longer had the power to give readings or séances or use Ouija boards. I burned everything that associated itself to the dark side of life. Satan's powers were gone. The Holy Spirit truly made the difference in my life. Now I could read the Bible with understanding in truth, because the spirit within me opened up areas where I had never walked. The Bible came alive. Jesus was real. Hell, brimstone and fire were a reality. Heaven was as certain as I was breathing.

And to think I almost died believing in what I was doing. Hell would have been my eternity. Thank You, Jesus, for sending me to a church that preached hell, brimstone and fire. As much as I have loved my mother, I'm sorry she was wrong. Not every church is going to Heaven. I was able to lead my mother and father to Jesus. I was the first in my family to receive Jesus, and others followed.

My experiences reach to others who are where I was. Jesus loves you. Like I once did, many believe after selling out to Satan that they no longer can turn away and be forgiven. This is a lie from the pits of Hell. You can change masters, and you too can be transformed. Have faith, trust and believe. Speak to that controlling spirit of Satan within you: I say to you, I close your ears, eyes, and mouth. You no longer have power over this child. I pray God, send your angels to get Satan and his demons so far away from the readers that they cannot see, hear, or speak to them. Now to you, reader, I say trust and believe, and pray this prayer with me.

Jesus, I believe you died on the cross for me. I ask you to forgive me of my sins and come into my heart. Make me the person you want me to be. Not what I want, but what you want. Thank you, Jesus, for coming into my life. Now use my past to help others. Use me in any way you see fit. I'm yours.

Now, find a gospel-preaching, Bible-toting church.

Now if you meant this prayer like I did when I prayed it, the angels in Heaven are singing, your name is written in the Book of Life, and you are my brother or sister. Praise God! Now tell others of your changed life and go into the highways and byways and bring the lost to Christ. Game time is over.

When I was saved, I had a real burden for the youth of our town. The communities around us had no outlet for teen involvement. They needed the true love of Christians that could reach beyond their hurts and pains of life. If we could only get a place for recreational games and people willing to take time to listen to the needs of their children. I went to the adults in the church with no response. I tried to get an empty building in town, with no help. I didn't want to see the lives of these youth overlooked as Darrell's life had been. Nothing I tried worked. It seemed no one cared. I felt like one person in a desert of darkness. My hands were tied. I would go uptown with my red Volkswagen. I was told later that when the teens saw my car come into town, they would scatter. "Warning, everyone, here comes the preacher on wheels." I would park the car close to the corner in town and slowly the youth began to trust me and would come to my car and talk to me. They talked about their family lives, and one-on-one I would love on these teens, and they began opening up. I wanted to see Darrell involved in spiritual things. I started with the youth. Darrell never joined us, but I didn't give up. I knew these youth were into drugs and alcohol, and I wanted to pat their hands and say, "You know, you shouldn't do that."

I guess I really didn't know how to handle this, until my eyes and ears were opened to reality. One of the youth came to me and told me that she needed to talk to me. She said several of the youth were doing drugs in an abandoned house and one of the girls cried out to her for help. She laughed at her. This girl cried out for help from another, and they laughed at her again. The girl's body was in seizures. She couldn't talk clearly, and she became lifeless. Someone screamed, "She's dying," and out of fear of the law, the youth all left, and the next day her body was found. She had died.

God spoke to me directly then: Stop playing games, I'm soon in coming.

My life has been transformed and game time is over. Only the truth will set us free. I serve a risen Savior, and His blood on the cross is the answer to lead us to eternal bliss.

The transformation in my life is nothing more than the life Jesus lived on this earth. I have a long way to go, but I want my life to count, my experiences to mean something to help those who are like gasping fish out of water. My goal in this book and in my life is to pass on what I have learned, and put the people who are floundering back into the life-giving tank of living water that is Jesus Christ. I want to give hope to the hopeless and build God's Kingdom. We can do all things if we have faith and believe.

I'm in a battle, and my enemies are Satan and his demons. Jesus said if I have faith the size of a mustard seed, I can move mighty mountains. I have a mind set to believe just that. The word of God says when we see Satan, we will wonder why we ever feared him. The power is in the tongue. Greater is He that is in me than he who is in the world. I can do all things through Christ who strengthens me. God is looking for warriors who dare stand for what is right, Soldiers of God who truly know the King.

The battleground is the mind; Satan can only put thoughts in a Christian's mind. He no longer can know what you think, because he no longer has occupancy. He may put thoughts in the mind, but without action on our part, he doesn't have puppets any longer.

Let me tell you, I have found my walk with Christ has been very deep, and my worst enemies have been Christians. Why is it that when God tells you to do something and you stick to it, the Christians are the ones who throw water on the fire? I heard it said and I believe it, that Christians are the only army that buries its wounded alive. I'm a God-pleaser, not a man-pleaser, and when God speaks, I listen and obey. I have stood alone in decisions and have had even pastors come against me, and then later after all was said and done, these same people who believe lies told to them about the brethren say they are sorry. My response to those who listen to gossip is that you need to go to God for the answers and not depend on what people choose to believe. I do.

At the time my heart was transformed, so was my mind. I know God's voice and I will follow His lead. I graduated from a Christian college with a degree in ministerial ministries in 1990. On the night of my graduation, I went forward for prayer, and was unable to stay for the celebration. After prayer, I left with a loaded trailer that we took to the Appalachian Mountains. I was born to help and to serve people in need. God told me to feed and clothe the needy, and they will come to Him. This is happening. I know I may fall short, but my hero is Jesus and I want to be as much like Jesus as I can.

CHAPTER 6

THE MOMENT I MET GOD

It wasn't hard leaving my old ways, because I had a new master, a new leader. My mind and heart had changed; the lies of Satan no longer controlled me. The Bible says the truth will set you free. Luke 16 tells the story of the rich man who wanted for nothing, and the poor man only asked for the crumbs off the table of the rich man. The poor man believed in God and went to Paradise (Heaven); the rich man rejected God and went to Hades (Hell). How close I was to Hell. Only God knows.

All the time I served Satan, I thought I was serving God in Heaven. How could such power come upon anyone unless it was 'Big G' God? When I accepted Christ Jesus as Savior, I felt 50 pounds drop from my left shoulder. My salvation brought me into a new light, and God renewed me at that very moment. The power of giving readings was gone; the desire to do this was dissolved. For the first time in my life of serving under Satan, I was totally free. God carried me through when I could have been mincemeat in Satan's grip. I was now made whole in my creator's hands.

God was molding me in the clay of my experience to reach out to others who had fallen in a trap just as I had. I have such a compassion for those in the occult. I would like to see them set free, just as I was. This gift of salvation set me free, and it's there for the taking. Jesus is calling to you, reader. You may think you are so deep, you have sold out to Satan, and you have no hope. Let me tell you, this is a lie from the pits of hell. You can never go so deep that God will not pull you out and save you if you are truly repentant. It doesn't matter if you have sacrificed human beings, eaten their flesh, and drunk their blood: God will forgive you if only you ask. Your only hope is Jesus and what He did on the cross for you.

Saul was one of the worst. He thought he was doing a great thing to serve God, killing Christians. See how Satan had him in the clutches of his hands. Acts 22:3. Saul was zealous toward God. He persecuted to the death, delivering men and women followers of Jesus, verse 5 says, to be punished. He thought he was helping the cause of God, until he was on the road to Damascus, where he was blinded and a voice said, 'Saul, Saul, why do you persecute me?' Saul answered, 'Who are you, Lord?" and he said in verse 9, 'I am Jesus of Nazareth, whom you persecute.' Saul was blinded, but for the first time he saw the light. When He received his sight, he was called to witness of the true and Holy Jesus. He knew who Jesus was. My God, my God, what torture these beloved brothers went through. Thousands of people died in the name of making the world a better place by destroying Christians. When Saul met God on the road to Damascus, his life was changed. I had my Damascus Road when I heard the teaching on Hell, brimstone and fire for the first time, and I was set free. My blinded eyes were spiritually opened. God forgave me of all those things I was involved in, that I mistakenly thought were right.

God is waiting to forgive you, to wash your past clean, and when you truly ask for forgiveness and invite Jesus into your life, you too will receive a new heart. All that you have been through will only be building blocks to help others. Jesus is calling. Just as He called me out of darkness into the light, He is calling you. His love is so pure and great, and serving God has been the frosting on the cake. We are all born for a purpose, and what we do with our life will determine our destination for eternity, Hell or Heaven, God or Satan, the choice is ours.

There is nothing hidden that will not be uncovered at the judgment. The time is now. Putting our past, present, and future in the loving hands of Jesus will wipe away all we have done, and give rebirth to not Saul, but now Paul, who became one of the greatest

Apostles. He learned the truth and was set free. His life counted for the true love of God.

Remember, everything we go through was on the cross with Jesus. He suffered our sins so that we could go free.

Thank God, He was with me all the time I was in sin. He's here right now with you. He loves you and He's waiting. Here's a simple prayer that you can say.

God, I'm sorry I sinned. Jesus, I believe you died on the cross for me and I ask you to forgive me of all my wrongdoing and come into my life. Thank you, Jesus, for saving me.

If you have done this, your name is written in the Lamb's Book of Life. The angels are singing and you are now in the family of God. Welcome, brother and sister.

CHAPTER 7

TRANSFORMING MIND

My Grandfather Serrels loved his flower garden, and I believe his passion for seeing the beauty of those God-given gifts has been passed on to me.

I have a cut-out of Jesus praying in front of my garden. He kneels by a rock. I have taken pictures of my flowers, and in the developed photo I find Jesus' head is bowed and flowers have grown up to his nose, and it looks like He is smelling them. I call my garden the Jesus garden. It's unbelievable how beautiful the flowers are. In fact, my house burned in 2000, and while it was burning, people across the road kept remarking on the beauty of the flowers. The firemen never crushed one flower in the garden while they put out the fire.

While I was working in my garden, God spoke to me about the flowers. He said these flowers are like people. "They need manure to grow. Without fertilizer, they will be puny and unhealthy. It's through trials and trusting me that you grow. The same way the fertilizer grows the flowers, trials will grow you and put you in all the places where I can use you." I was going through great trials at that time, and I said, "Yes, God, and I'm up to my knees in dung, thank you."

No sarcasm meant here, only truth and reality. I have seen the picture. I hope you have. Although pansies are a beautiful flower, as God-fearing Christians, we do not want to have the name of pansy. Maybe we should think of ourselves as tall, wide-brim sunflower heads. Look at all the seeds they produce. Toil and work are the keys. As we grow in our trouble, we can reproduce in Jesus' footsteps.

This song comes to me:

> *Step into the waters*
> *Wade out a little bit deeper.*

This is referring to trusting the Holy Spirit to do His work in us. The water represents the Holy Spirit, and what started out in fear is a refreshing savor in God's love. I guess that's my way of expressing the love of Jesus.

I have grown so much in the Lord. I once had hate in my heart for those who crossed me. By learning to give thanks in all things (Ephesians 5:20, I Thessalonians 5:18), I have matured and forgiven them. Jesus said if we don't forgive, He won't. It's too much of a burden on anyone's heart to have unforgiveness; this causes sickness and even death. It's not worth it to harbor resentment, bitterness, and hatred. It's not worth it.

I am free from the life of Satan's destruction. He is out to get the Christians, to destroy the family and cause division. I have family members who have misused me, stabbed me in the chest and the back. At one time I wanted revenge, but not now. I love them, because I have given praise in the good and the bad, and this kind of love can only come from the Holy Spirit and the word applied to my heart.

I used to think I had to try to keep both sides of our family together, but it never worked. Unless God builds new relationships and people truly want to serve Him, hearts will never change. So I just stay away from those who claim to be Christians, and yet do not love their neighbor. Thank you, Jesus, that I have family members who reject me, who have misused me. This is part of another growing process. I put you, Father, Jesus, first in my life. For your word tells me that father will turn against son, mother against daughter, and I see it around me. I'm living it, and that's okay. I just ask You in Your timing that You will change things. I put You first in my life. Your will be done.

CHAPTER 8

DROPPING OFF OLD WAYS

How does your garden grow? With trials, tribulations, hurts, and pain; that's how my garden grows. With toil and dirt and the gardener through Jesus, the Holy Spirit, that's how my garden grows.

When you accept Jesus Christ's deliverance and truly follows His leading, you can do nothing but grow. You see, it's the Holy Spirit within that teaches, leads, and directs, and when we obey, there will be no more misgivings.

Along with Darrell, Teresa has told me that I am a mean mother, and so be it. Teresa acted out from the deep wounds of her innocence being stolen. I found out about Teresa's molestation in her senior year. After Bill and I separated, he moved 10 miles away. Teresa told me some of the things that had happened to her. I wanted to kill Bill. I looked for the pistol that was once in our home, but it was gone. Bill had come in and taken it. My thoughts were to go out and shoot and kill him, and turn the gun on myself. Thank God, the gun was gone. I have never in all my life since then wanted to kill anyone. Since Teresa's actions as a child, I'm very sensitive to those acting out in rebellion, and have been able to help others who are struggling with bad behavior. I write this as a parent who didn't understand, and I tell you, reader parents, rebellion is sometimes a deeper cause than what it looks like.

I love my children and grandchildren very much, but I have let go through many days of crying, praying and struggling with separation from Wendell, Tamara and Billy. Since their marriages and the divorce, they have all gone their own separate ways. What I dreamed of when the children were growing up was to have family reunions here at the house, but as each child and their spouses make choices, I have to let go and let God. Thanking God in all these things once again has given me peace, knowing God knew all these happenings, the lies spoken. I'm not alone. I have the Father, Son , and the Holy Ghost. They even let me know in advance the things said, and later it comes back to me what is spoken. When we trust God, we have it all.

I don't even want to think of what my life would be if I didn't have Jesus as Savior. I remember what my life was like before salvation, when Satan was my father. He was leading me down death's road, the wide road to Hell. In the beginning, everything was great, but when the devil is finished with you, he will destroy you. He tried to destroy me, but did not succeed. Praise God!

When I received Jesus as Savior, I didn't know anything about the Bible. I had to determine to study, to hide God's work in my heart. I had to decide to be a follower, to be a soldier of the cross, to stand firm with the Chief Commander. I started out on the milk; you cannot feed newborns meat until they have first been on the bottle. Babies will get sick if given solids too fast, then they will throw up. That's the same with the growth of every new Christian. I Timothy 2:6 says do not promote novices into office, lest being lifted up with pride, they fall to the condemnation of the dead. This to me is very sound advice. When I first received Christ as Savior, the church I started attending had very few grown-ups to be teachers. These people were determined I would teach Sunday school. I was just as determined not to, until I got in the Word. I needed to know what I was teaching. Had I gotten into teaching, knowing nothing, I'm sure I would have gotten prideful and could have been destroyed as a novice.

Today, I'm no longer a novice. Through my trials, I have become stronger than ever. God's word is so real and true, my life is and has been changed. Thank You, Jesus.

In 2003, we were headed for the Appalachian Mountains, taking a load of needed items, clothes, food, and furniture in the truck that I had bought with my inheritance money. While riding, I was getting

SATAN WANTS ME, GOD HAS ME.

sick, I was in pain, but I said nothing to the driver. I had cashed in my life insurance and bought a church out there, and it had been advertised that we would be having a giveaway. When we got there, I sat quietly in a pew knowing, I was having a heart attack. Again, I said nothing. People came in and I prayed with them. When I got home, I stayed in the apartment for two weeks. I sat in a chair having chest pain. The ladies who were running God's mission outreach – a warehouse in Maple Rapids, Michigan, where every Tuesday people would bring in clothes, food and household items – would sort, box, and stack these items to wait for a semi to pick and deliver them to the Appalachian Mountains. These ladies would come in from boxing up clothes and miscellaneous and tell me to go to the doctor. I said I would when God told me.

That night, I spoke on the phone to one of the brothers from the Appalachian Mountains. He said, "Sister Cora, you get to the doctor. We need you here." I didn't say anything.

After the call I said, "God, if I'm in as much pain tomorrow as I have been, I will go to the doctor, if You set up an appointment." I called the next day, set up an appointment, and went into the doctor's office. When the doctor walked in, he didn't even check me.

He said, "You get to the Emergency Room right now and don't stop anywhere."

When I got there, they took me right into a bed, brought a machine that tested for a heart attack, and then the doctor came in and gave me a shot for a blood clot on my heart.

I said, "Praise the Lord, it doesn't matter anyhow."

I said, "Praise the Lord, it doesn't matter anyhow."

I was taken to a bigger hospital by ambulance, and when we arrived, the driver asked the attendant what my EKG was. He said two or three.

I asked what he was talking about, and he said I had had two to three heart attacks.

I said, "Okay. Praise the Lord, it doesn't matter anyhow."

I was taken to the only bed available at that hospital, and the heart specialist came in right away. He told me I had one to three plugged arteries, 85 to 95%.

I said, "Okay. Praise the Lord, it doesn't matter anyhow."

He said they would have to balloon stint and I would have heart damage.

I said, "Okay. Praise the Lord, it doesn't matter anyhow."

The nurse popped in and said the surgeons wanted me down to surgery right away. They had taken someone else out and put me in their place. I got downstairs, and a young man came in and said he was going to be my nurse. I said okay.

He looked at my name and hollered out, "Cora Goldman, I know you."

I said, "Who are you?" He told me I used to be his second grade Sunday school teacher.

We got in the surgical room and he told the people there I was a good Christian woman. The doctor came in ask who the patient was. When they told him, he said he knew me, and he asked me how. I said I don't know how he knew me, I just lay there, thanking God, asking for no pain and no complications, just praying and praising.

When they finished the surgery, the doctor said he couldn't believe it: there was only one artery blocked at 30%. That night, my son called from work and said he was bringing alcohol and salve to make sure I didn't get infection. I told him not to, because I couldn't find the incision. He came anyhow. He couldn't find the incision, nor could his girlfriend. He threw his arms in the air and left.

When I went back to my regular doctor, he said he couldn't believe I had had a heart attack. I had a brand new, perfect heart.

In all things, give thanks.

Does God always heal? NO. Sometimes, I believe, we have to go through stuff for growth.

One year to the date of all this hospital activity, while in West Virginia, I injured my back. When I got home, I went to the doctor. For two months, I went to the doctor and was on pain meds, with no relief. I thanked God, and I know when I couldn't walk, He carried me.

The doctor walked into the room at his office where I waited, and said, "Cora you're not a complainer. There is something wrong. I'm sending you in for an MRI."

I was told I had several ruptured discs, numbers 2, 3 and 4, where the jelly was coming out, and I would need surgery. I could hardly walk, the pain was so bad. I kept praying, asking God for healing.

I was just so sure I was going to receive a new back, the way I had received a new heart the year before. But God had other plans. I could have received a healing, but God's plans are above man's. I was sent to a neurosurgeon, and on December 2nd I was put in the hospital. I spent the night and was released after my surgery and one night of stay. I could no longer sleep in my bed. It was too hard, so I adopted the couch. The only time I got up was to go to the bathroom and kitchen. It didn't seem like the pain was going away, but I just felt it was due to the surgery and I would get better.

Let me tell you, there was no getting better. In fact, one day while I was alone, the pain was so bad, I screamed for God's help to get me back to the couch. I called the neurologist and he told me to come in. Another MRI found discs 3 and 4 had not been removed. Thank You, Jesus.

On February $3^{rd,}$ I was sent to have another surgery. I spent the night at the hospital, and the next day they asked me about my left side. I said that was okay, but my right side was having pain. Another MRI found I had a ruptured disc on the right side now. I was in the hospital pretty much the month of February. I was released to go home, and a day-and-a-half later was back in the hospital with a staff infection. Now I'm on a drip for the infection. Thank You, Jesus.

A pick line was put in, and on the day I was released to go home, the pick line was removed. Thank You, Jesus.

Three days later, I was taken back to the hospital because the pain in my arm was so bad I couldn't move it. An ultrasound found a blood clot five inches long, headed for my lungs. A doctor and the technician said I had gotten in just in time. Praise the Lord.

Hebron was given to me to stop the growth, and then coumadin. On the day I was to go home, blood started pouring out of me. Thank You, Jesus.

I ended up staying. Things seemed to be under control, and after I was home a few days, I had a stroke. My face contorted, my eye drooped, and my speech slurred. So I ended in the hospital again. Thank You, Jesus. In all I go through, I know I'm being tested, but You and I together, we can do it.

People all over and in different states have been praying for me. I could feel it. By the way, the stroke did not leave me with any problems. Thank You, Jesus.

My stay in the hospital opened doors and allowed me to lead 11 people to the Lord, including a doctor and nurse and aides, along with roommates. What Satan means for evil, God will turn around for good. I love You, Father, Jesus, and Holy Spirit. Thank You so much.

Greater is He who is in you than he who is in the world. If we can get hold of the scripture and truly apply it to our lives, we can move mighty mountains. All it takes is a mustard seed-sized faith to grow mighty trees that even house birds and animals. One seed, just one tiny seed can change lives. For in the last days, Acts says, God will pour out His Spirit upon all flesh. Your sons and daughters shall prophesy, your young men shall have visions, your old men shall have dreams.

Jesus said He will pour His Spirit out in the end days. I don't know about you, but I want all of the Holy Spirit I can have. I can do nothing without the Holy Spirit. He directs me, and has never let me stray.

While in the Appalachian Mountains I was told of a young mother in Intensive Care. When I went to see her, she was all swollen up and couldn't talk.

I told her, "This was Sister Cora," and asked if I could pray with her.

She told me later she thought she had died and gone to Heaven, because Sister Cora wouldn't come from Michigan to pray for her. I anointed her with olive oil just as God had spoken to me to do many times before. I spoke against death, and spoke life.

Within a short time, she said, "It's going, it's going, the pain is going." The next day, they transferred her to a regular room.

I was at a mission, dropping off furniture, clothing, miscellaneous, and she was there. When she saw me, she called to her two boys and told them who I was. They both came running. Each one took hold and hugged a leg.

Her mama said, "You know she was dying, don't you?"

I said, "Yes, I do." She said the news of the miracle was going all over the mountains.

SATAN WANTS ME, GOD HAS ME.

Becky came to me and said she had to go back to the doctor in two weeks, because he said she was full of stones. We anointed her and prayed to destroy the stones in the name of Jesus Christ. When she met went back to the doctor, they looked three times and found no stones. They were upset and sent her home.

I can do nothing without the leading of God, Jesus, and the Holy Spirit. I am sold out to the service of the Kingdom, and He wants to use every one. He wants to use you. People need to see the power of God in the church, and the church is every individual who has accepted Christ Jesus as Savior. You've got the power. Let go and let God.

I was invited to visit the home of a family of four. All four asked Jesus into their hearts. For 20 years, the father was in pain and could hardly walk. I anointed and prayed for him, and this big man cried.

I said, "What's the matter?"

He said, "It's hot in there."

I said, "God's healing you."

He was able to walk for the first time without pain. When I got home, I was told God had given him a new kneecap, and he was all over showing the people.

We've seen cancer healed, and cripples walk. A lady had such heart problems, she had only a few weeks to live. We prayed for her, and at her next appointment, x-rays found she had a brand new heart.

Jacob, a young man of 23, was found in a coma in the front yard of his parents' home. For three weeks, he was on life support. I was asked to go up to the hospital to pray with him. His mother met me in the hallway, and as we were talking, suddenly I knew I had to go in and pray with him.

Looking at Jacob's lifeless body, I said, "Jacob, this is Aunt Cora. Now you listen to what I say, and do what I tell you. God is going to speak to you. You do what He says."

Jacob's nose twitched, he moved, his nostrils flared, the first sign of life. I then came against the spirit of death and spoke life. His stomach jumped. The nurse told us we had to leave, because the doctor was coming in to try to figure out the surgery procedures to remove the cement-like hardness that had formed in his lungs. By the time the doctor got into the hospital room, they took 10 liters of liquid off his lungs. They called Jacob their miracle boy.

Three weeks later, after church, I had a message on my phone: "Aunt Cora, this is Jacob. Give me a call."

I did call. "Jacob, did you hear me talk to you while you were in the coma?"

"Yes, and at that time my spirit was going up a tube to a bright light. I pounded on the brightly lit door. A man dressed in white came to the door with a dove on his shoulder and told me to go back. I did, and my stomach jumped that night."

Remember, people in comas hear all you say. Those that I shared are just a small number of healings.

God is still on the throne. He is the same today and forever. He doesn't change. Let's let God be God and follow His direction and His leading, and there will be many more miracles. This book would not contain all God has done in the ministry He has given me. Ask God to use you, and be ready to be used.

CHAPTER 9

MATURITY

Oh yeah, I've had them. Struggles that is. I know Satan would like me to be destroyed. I have to come against Satan and his demons on a daily basis. Knowing God is in it, allowing me to trust Him and with me, He will fight the battle, for I am on the winning side. I've read the last book in the Bible. I know who wins.

It seems every since my salvation, spiritually the battle has been on. I've heard it said that with salvation, you can rest, with no troubles. What a lie. When I changed my father from Satan to God, I have had even the Christians come against me. It's been a challenge. Greater is Jesus who is in us, than Satan who's in the world.

Life has always been a struggle, as I have already shared with some stories of my childhood. Even when I didn't know God, He was in it. Thank You, Jesus. He knew me when I didn't know Him. He loved me when I didn't love Him. How wonderful His love.

I remember buying dresses for Mother and me at the variety store in Bannister. I babysat, and earned $.35 per hour to buy those dresses. Mother and I went to a PTA dance, and I sat against the wall like a wallflower. I wanted someone to ask me to dance, and then I didn't, because my self-esteem was so low. I never felt good enough for anyone, even me.

When Bill asked me to marry him, I felt like someone truly loved me and wanted me for me. I felt that God, even though I had no personal relationship with Him, had put Bill and me together. As time went on and the babies began to come, Bill had several affairs on me. I always forgave, believing God was going to change things. Life was a struggle, being married and not knowing what love was even then. When I married, I married for a lifetime. When I said 'I do,' I meant it. I believe all that we go through was nailed onto the cross with Jesus, and all things are possible.

Life was a struggle with my in-laws, who tried to break up our marriage. Everything I have gone through has made me a better person. I can now relate to those who are going through what I've been through.

When I accepted Christ Jesus as my personal savior, my life was totally changed. I'm not a man-pleaser, I'm a God-pleaser. I know God's voice, and even when I stand alone, God stands with me.

We had an open house for the mission, with missionaries visiting, and it was a terrible time. Untrue things were said. My two daughters were devastated. They left, and I was left with five people who came against me big time. When they made terrible accusations and I asked who told them such things, their only response was that the information came from a reliable source, but they wouldn't give any names. God spoke to me one name: Jane. I asked Jane if she was telling people such things, and she said my attitude refers to these untruths. I am not sure what she meant when she said this. I had made no changes, but it was a set-up, to come against the mission work, to try to take over what these people came in to help with. Those who chose to believe without checking truth were, I believe, ambitious. There have been many wolves in sheep's clothing who have tried on their own to start mission work, and these people failed in their venture to take over because God was letting me know in advance who my enemy was. I faced this issue and didn't cower down. I let go and let God, and with truth He took care of wagging tongues. God told me to telephone Jane. I'm a confronter, and all was uncovered and the truth came out.

It really is a life of struggles, trying to serve God. This earth is a battlefield of spiritual deceptions. We are not fighting against flesh and blood, but against principalities, against powers and rulers of darkness of this world, against spiritual wickedness in high places.

God's word says to test the spirits to know they are of God. Even those who call themselves Christian can be deceivers.

Being a Christian and standing for truth and not bending is not popular. I don't care to be popular to man. One day, each one of us will give account for what we have done. We will stand before Jesus. I am not perfect; I strive to be like Jesus. If I make enemies of those who walk a crooked path, then so be it.

We've had some very well known people who have tried to take over the mission, but again, I told them when God speaks to me to do something, don't stand in my way. I'm like a bull in a china store; I will knock them over. Well, guess what? These people don't like me. But God loves me, and that is what matters to me. Just because people hold offices does not justify stealing, lying, and cheating. God see it all, and what is done in darkness will be revealed in the light. Jesus said He would rather you be hot or cold. If you are lukewarm, you will be spewed out of His mouth. In other words, He will throw up.

We've had people selling things that were given to the Appalachian Mountains to hand out free. People have been misused. Eight groups received clothes, food and miscellaneous furniture to freely give to those in need, but instead they charged people for those things. I take seriously the commission God has put before me. If people are not honest in their dealings, I can't work with them. I can't be a man-pleaser and please God at the same time. I've made enemies because I want honesty. One of the 10 Commandments says you shall not steal. My mother hated lying, and she said if you lie, you'll steal. I say if you are a liar, you steal from the truth. If we love the Lord with all our heart, we won't want to hurt Him or our neighbor. Stand for what's right, and you'll never have to be ashamed.

When my husband divorced me, he was married two days later. That was okay. If this made him happy, then so be it. My youngest son and I were very close, but as he was growing up, he decided to desert me and go to his father and stepmother. I cried. I was heartbroken. Then I heard later my ex had told the boys stories that weren't true.

Many a night, I struggled with the last three of my children. Then I applied praise: Ephesians 5:20, I Thessalonians 5:18, in everything give thanks. Thank You, God, that my children have departed from me. But You take care of it.

I began to get strength and peace filled my being. Now it was okay that the stepmother took the place of the biological mother. It was okay that these children had no place for me in their lives. Then God let me see something. I had always been there loving my children. Bill had never paid attention to the children. They needed his love. They didn't have to compete for my love.

One of my big hurts and struggles was hearing of Bill going places with his new wife, when he wouldn't go out with me. Thank You, Jesus. I've been made a new person, just praising God in my trials and struggles.

Seven months after their marriage, Bill was found dead on the couch. My daughter and I went to the funeral. I never bawled so hard. Seeing this man's body in a casket and 37-1/2 years wiped out. This man never asked my daughter's forgiveness for the years he had molested her, or my forgiveness for the hurts, the pains, the women, the destruction that tore our family apart. It was always my dream, as my children were growing up, that when they became adults with families of their own, we would always be together, having barbecues and holidays, and watching the grandchildren grow up. I never knew how dysfunctional our family was. I thought we were a perfect family. How wrong I was. I guess the trait of dysfunction has been passed on to all my children. Everyone has their own trials and troubles, and we all have to work them out the best we know how. Mine is just praising God and thanking Him. Without troubles and trusting God, we would never grow spiritually. All things work together for good to those who love the Lord, those called according to His purpose.

CHAPTER 10

GROWTH

I can do nothing without God the Holy Spirit. I am nothing without Jesus Christ, but I am somebody with the Holy Spirit in me. My last name is now Christian. I belong to the Father, Jesus Christ.

When my youngest was five years old, he took very sick. For three days, I took care of him, thinking he had the flu. A neighbor man could only find comfort from pain when he sat up, so I slept with Billy and sat him up against the wall, and he did all right. When he would slide down, he would cry in pain. After the third day, God said to take him to the doctor now, so I did.

The doctor said, "Do you mind putting him in the hospital?"

I said, "No! What do you think it is?"

Appendix, he said. The snow was falling when we finally made it to the hospital and he was given a bed in pediatrics. My husband called and told me to come home because they needed me. I said no! Billy needed me. I had made a promise to myself, if any of my children were ever hospitalized, I would stay with them. I couldn't when Barry Lynn was dying. I wasn't allowed. Billy needed me, and I wasn't going to leave him.

Billy was in awful pain. The shots didn't help, and the staff said they were sure he had the flu and not appendix. My baby couldn't find any rest, and then it hit me.

"Billy, can you say the Lord's prayer with me?"

Together we prayed, *Our Father, which art in Heaven,* and it was like a sedative. Billy went sound asleep. The next morning he was running a low temperature, and they decided to do surgery. The doctor talked to me afterward and said Billy's appendix had ruptured. They gave him a 50-50 chance of making it. Later, they told me they didn't expect him to make it. There were six doctors and nurses working over this lifeless little body. I watched through a glass window, begging God not to take his life.

"God, You've taken one of my children, please don't take another."

Then this thought came to me: Cora, don't beg God. Thank Him.

"Oh! God, I'm sorry, forgive me. Thank you, God, that you've taken one of my children." Actually, no child belongs to us, they are only loaned to us to raise, to teach and to direct. "Lord, I give this child to You. If it is Your will to take him, he is Yours. You know best."

Within a short time, this lifeless body was moving and the staff was jumping around. The doctor then told me it was possible within a few days, Billy's incision would develop an abscess. If this happened and they were to put a needle in the abscess, draw out the poison, and shoot it in a dog, it would kill the dog instantly.

I had been at the hospital for a couple days, so I went home, leaving Billy playing and happily riding a tricycle in the hospital. They called him their miracle baby. What we feared happened, and he was taken into emergency surgery. Again I began praising God, and thanking Him in the death bed reality of the circumstance facing us.

"God, I thank You, but you can change things."

Prayer changes things. Thanking God gives Him control. I said again to the hospital staff, my baby was going to be all right. I went home, and when I went up to see Billy the next day – remember, he was only five years old – he said, "Mama, guess who was here to see me?"

"I don't know, honey, who was?"

"God was here."

"What did he look like, honey?"

"I don't know. I couldn't see His face, but He talked to me."

"What did he say?"

"I don't know, but He talked to me. He sent me a rabbit that sat outside my window and I'm going to be okay."

My best Christmas. God gave back to me what Satan tried to take. Thank You, Jesus.

I had a Siamese cat named Susie. One day while the children were at my mother's, I heard a noise in the bathroom. Here the cat was sitting on my third child's potty chair. I saved the stool to show my husband.

He said, "Pretty good. The kid goes on the floor, and the cat on the pot."

Then the cat started using the big toilet, and Wendell used to sit on the potty watching the cat. Susie potty-trained my son. What an amazing cat. We had her for a lot of years.

It was a cold day when Susie lay limp on the porch, dying. My husband came in, took a look at the cat, and went back outside. Darrell suggested we put the cat in the warm bathroom to let her die. I agreed. She was put in a box and we left her alone. Suddenly, the Bible came alive to me. Jesus healed the sick and dying, and He said we could do the same. We loved our cat, and God said He would give us the desires of our heart. I went and got the box with our lifeless Susie. My five children and I stood around the box, praying.

"God, You see Susie. She's almost dead. You said You give us the desires of our heart, and we would like life back into our pet. You see the sparrows when they fall. We plead the blood of Jesus for life over and through the animal."

We put her back into the bathroom, and within a few minutes, Susie walked out very much alive. She didn't look like she had had such a close call.

Bill came in, asking where the cat was. He said, "What did you do?"

"We prayed for her."

He said, "You had no business. I had the hole dug."

If I shared all the miracles and prayers that God has answered, it would take several volumes. I hope these stories will help you the reader to realize how much God truly cares about our needs and about those things that are close to our hearts. God wants to use you,

He wants to use me. So begin to practice on the same things I have, and when you build positive prayer, believing God can do what He says He wants to in you, then you can go to people, just as I have.

God had spoken to me to promote gospel music. I said, "God, I don't know how." He said, "I will teach you." He did, and we were able to get established groups to go into parks and schools and have concerts to win souls. Everything was free. God said to get tax exempt, and showed me how to do that. As I listened to the Spirit, then acted upon the voice of God, everything worked out.

We had set up a gospel concert in a park, with three groups that would be playing. I was with one of the members from the band when my nephew brought me a gopher on a paper plate. It was stiff and fleas were jumping off it.

He said, "Aunt Cora, I seen its eyes blink. It's still alive."

I guess I didn't pay any attention to the rigor mortis that had taken over. I cupped my hand over the little animal and pled the blood of Jesus, asking life and not death. Praising God for the dying animal, asking God to give life, I repeated this prayer for more than half an hour. I believed God's word says ask and ye shall receive. There were two of us praying. I thought this woman with me believed life could be brought back into this animal, but she told me later she was talking to God and asking Him what she was doing here with a crazy woman, praying life into a dead gopher. I believe things happen for a reason, and in God's timing. We were walking up to the stage and the most incredible thing happened in front of the woman and others. I felt life moving under my hand, and as I released my hand to see, this gopher jumped from the paper plate unto the stage and ran off into the grass. People were in awe. They saw a miracle of God.

Don't give up. Keep believing. If you stand alone, so be it. I'd rather stand with God, knowing His work and what He can do and wants to do with me, than hear the Fatherless cries of unbelief. If Jesus is for you, who can be against you?

My daughter used to baby-sit for a woman named Connie, and we became good friends. One day at her house, we knelt in her entryway and she asked Jesus into her heart. This woman has spun out of her cocoon and is dynamite for the kingdom of God.

She's a teacher, leader and a spokesman for God, saving souls for the Kingdom. What an awesome woman.

Connie had moved onto a farm, where her husband was a dairy man. They had milkers, babies, and hundreds of stock. Every day they were losing the calves and cows to death. I told Connie I would come over while her husband was gone and pray for each animal. I took my bottle of olive oil, making a cross on each head, pleading the blood of Jesus Christ over them, and speaking life instead of death. This was my friend and sister in the Lord's livelihood. Do you know, from that time, death was destroyed. Not another animal died. What's important to you is very much important to God.

This reminds me of friends who were raising dogs to help pay bills. The puppies had gotten parvo and began dying. The day I went to their house, the puppies were all sick. I did the same thing with the oil. I anointed the puppies and prayed life and not death, pleading the blood of Jesus Christ for healing. God did the rest. This earth is only a training ground to do bigger and better things, so come on aboard. God wants to use you. Let Him. He's a great teacher. Let go and let God.

I love trees. In fact, all but a couple of the trees in my yard, I planted. I purchased a plum tree for my husband for Father's Day. While there at the store, I saw a dead stick that had been thrown away, and ask the salesperson if I could have it. He said they couldn't give anything away, they had to sell it. I paid two cents for it, went home and planted the $15 plum tree, and then asked Bill where to plant the dead stick. I planted it right where he said. For two weeks, every day I went out to this dead stick in the ground and prayed over it, pleading the blood of Jesus, asking for life in this stick, reminding God that He sees and knows each sparrow that dies, and I know He can give life to this tree. What is impossible with man is very possible with God.

After two weeks, there was a leaf, and in time this dead stick began to flourish. I didn't know what this tree was, nor did the attendant at the store. Blossoms filled this tree as it grew, and we ended up with the most delicious fruit, a cross between an apricot and a peach. It makes the best jam. Well, my husband wanted to cut down my miracle tree because it was in the septic field.

I said, "That's where you told me to plant it."

"When I told you to plant it there, it was dead," he said. "I never expected it to grow like this."

Bill was very jealous of me, and I knew that was why he wanted to cut the tree down. The tree is close to 20 years old now, and has never given any trouble where it is.

God is full of miracles and He wants to use each one of us to let the world know He has not changed. He is still using people today to perform so many great works. How about it? Are you ready to go in the highways and byways, changing yourself by the powers of God? He needs your dedication and your abilities. Only through Him can we have strength peace and joy. Let go, and let God.

CHAPTER 11

STRUGGLES

We will always have those who will oppose us in our walk with Jesus. It doesn't matter if it's pastors, lay people, or whoever. God is still on the throne, and He can do anything He wants, with whoever He wants. All I can say is, if God said it, He will stand by you. Do it. He will bless you just as He has blessed me.

Some have joined cults and have sold out to Satan, giving him their souls. They are told they cannot change, that they are forever Lucifer's. Some have eaten human flesh, and even killed and drank the blood of those who once walked with them, and people tell them they can never get out of Satan's powers. This is a lie from Hell. Don't believe it.

The blood of Jesus is more powerful than any initiation of Satan. We all make choices. We have to live with them, or we can change those choices and turn our lives from evil to good. No matter what you have done in life, God loves you and Jesus died for you. You may think you are not worthy of forgiveness. Jesus says if you were the only person on Earth, He would have died for you. His blood is as alive today as it was on the cross, 2,000 years ago. I marvel over God's love for Saul, killing all those Christians in the name of the true Father. His life was totally changed when God confronted him with his persecution of His people. Right now, God is confronting you. How much time we have left before death or the return of Jesus for the church, no one but God knows. You are precious to God, and He wants you.

There are those who are prodigal children. Right now you may be hearing words or even thoughts from lying imps, telling you that you are not good enough. There is no one that is really good enough. It's the Grace of God that anyone can be saved. Don't keep beating on yourself, just let go. This is my prayer for you

In the name of Jesus Christ, I bind up enemy, lying spirits and loose the angels in Heaven to minister to you, the reader. I close the ears, eyes, and mouths of Satan and his demons. God, send your angels to get Satan and his demons so far away that they cannot see, hear, or speak. Now is the invitation to become the bride of Christ Jesus.

Men and women, pray this prayer with me:

God, I believe Jesus died for my sins. I am a sinner. I ask You to forgive me, and I invite Jesus to come live within me. Use me, Lord, to bring others to You. Make me the person You want me to be, and not what I want. Thank you, Jesus, for saving me.

If you meant this prayer, your past is as far from you as the east is from the west. God has wiped it from His memory, and now you need to ask help to forgive yourself and let God use you to help others into the kingdom. Remember always, God is only a prayer away.

CHAPTER 12

MIRACLES OF GOD

People who really want out can get out. But it takes the cross. The blood of Jesus is more powerful than anything Satan has to offer. When my youngest brother was about five years old, he would be playing with Tinker Toys and talking to someone, carrying on a conversation. We all thought it was just a game, but found out later through a medium that this was Howard's playmate, White Owl. Of course, this was a demon disguised as a friend. Fear at night crept into this child, but during the day, all was calmed.

Growing up, Howard was a loner, and when he was visited by a white owl, he had someone to talk to. He always got answers to any questions, he said, much like when he found God and talked to Him. At the time, everyone looked at this little demon friend as a welcomed visitor. During the day, he would play with his Tinker Toys and his electronic pieces to build with. His friend told Howard how to build working robots and how to build with his Tinker Toys. His little friend during daylight was very helpful and comforting.

Howard always had a hard time going to bed at night. It seemed at night and in the darkness there was evil all around him. Bedtime became an unwelcome enemy as he walked the stairs to his room. He recalls getting into bed, he felt something furry on his leg. He woke up to push the thing away, and the head hit his hands as he felt teeth pressing into him. Howard didn't link his daytime friend with his evening fright until his adulthood. Our family didn't know about Satan and his demons. We believed God was in all this. How will people know unless they are taught? How many families will go through this and not realize it is evil?

A young teenager and her friend were having troubles with dolls coming alive and walking and talking to them. The parents had heard about my helping people in deliverance, and got hold of me. The girl was scared to death of me at the first visit. Later, we found out that at the age of 13, she was suicidal. The dolls were telling her and her friend to commit suicide. Though this sounds bizarre, this is not my only case. We've had talking baby dolls, and pictures on walls that talked. Satan can and will do anything to get control of lives and destroy them. The teen burned all her dolls. She got saved and delivered and freed.

I remember a time when we left the spiritualist church meeting and I was visiting with an elderly lady outside the church. I felt an ant crawling on my arm and I killed it. "Oh, Cora," she said, "you shouldn't have killed that ant. It could have been a relative reincarnated." That blew me away. I had never heard such a thing, nor did I believe it. After my salvation and getting into the Bible, I read that Jesus was the only "reincarnated" person. He left Heaven to come to Earth as a baby to grow to manhood, to go to the cross for the sins of man. There is no new revelation. Jesus is the same today, tomorrow and forever. Revelation 22:7 says anyone adding to or taking from God's word will be given the plagues that are written in the Bible. There are many false prophets who come in the name of Jesus. Matthew 7:15 says beware of those false prophets who come in sheep's clothing. Jesus will come back the same as he left.

So many who call themselves Christians have turned to occult activity, saying there is nothing wrong with Dungeons and Dragons, Pokemon, hard rock music, some video games that kill the brain cells with murder, rape, all kinds of crimes, and with no remorse. I read the first Harry Potter book, and these books are no different from what I learned and once practiced in the spiritualist church. These are demons and come from the pit of Hell by the father of all lies and deceitful Satan and it's a wide road to Hell.

My friend Joan and our 96-year-Old shoe shorter from the mission went to Big Boy for dinner. Our waitress asked me if I was Cora, and I said yes. She asked if I knew who she was. When I said no, I didn't, she told me I was responsible for saving her life. She was the one with the talking dolls.

A young girl afraid for her life got hold of me. She used to play with her Ouija board as soon as she came home from school. One time, a demon wanted to come out of the board, and finally she let him. He started smashing up things in her room, and in fear she made him go back in. They tried to burn the boards without success. That was when I was called in. The girl got saved and delivered. We took the boards to the neighbors' burn barrel. We were determined to destroy the boards, and when they finally caught fire, the flames coming out of the board grew tall. The wind was blowing, and like hands the flames tried to grab her. I pushed her away, and contrary to the wind, the demon tried to get me. I jumped back, and the flames began burning oak leaves. Later I found out the girl was involved in the occult, that the symbol used was an oak tree. She was being prepared for sacrifice to Satan. We were able to give her the light. Years later, I met up with a friend of hers and asked how she was doing.

"She is married and has a little girl," the friend said. "She named her Grace."

"That is my middle name," I said.

"I know. She named her after you, because you saved her life."

I remember a young warlock being brought to me between two women. He had no strength before me and was weakened by the Spirit of God. Every time a demon came out, he got stronger. By the time the last demon came out, he stood up 6 feet. He picked me up in the air, put me down, and began shouting. He left the house saved and changed.

A young man had just mutilated his body before he came to me for deliverance. After his salvation and deliverance, he went to Teen Challenge. Satan is powerful, but God is the deliver and changer of life.

Years ago, I got a call from a grandmother who was having problems with demonic activity and her grandson. I met the father, mother and two teen girls outside on the porch. I told them I needed to know every opening in the house, such as attics. I also told the one girl I would do nothing until I knew they would destroy all the Satanic games, which kept them captive. She hated me. The whole family was sleeping on the floor, in fear of all the activity going on in the house. They had Christian radio in every room, 24 hours a day, with no relief.

We went through the house, anointing inside and out of every doorpost and bed, chasing the demons outside and to the place God had reserved for them. Then we pleaded the blood of Jesus over the inside and out of the house, putting out warring angels with swords drawn to do battle against any spirit that would try to destroy the family. When finished, we were in the kitchen, and the father spoke of a ceiling attic. I said we had to go and take care of that. There was a ladder, he stood on it, I dumped olive oil in his hands, and he threw oil all over in the attic. I told the demons to get out and sent them out the door to the place God had reserved for them. In the kitchen, the man told us that after I told the demons to get out, they hit him as they were leaving. Powerful, huh? That's God. Satan does not have power over God.

God has allowed me to help many who have been lied to, who were sold out to Satan, but now are free spirits in Jesus. I've been able to clean homes and churches where Satan once had rule. Nothing is impossible with God. You can get out, and you can get others out. This is your invitation to turn your life around and make it count.

CHAPTER 13

SPIRITUAL WARFARE

When men and women join any branch of the armed services, they must go through boot camp. It's the same in God's army, Earthly boot camp. Soldiers in the military are given weapons; they learn to use those weapons to save their lives and the lives of their comrades. If these soldiers pass qualifications, they will become property of the United States of America. Becoming a soldier in the service of God makes the Christians property of God, dying to self.

First of all, we as Christians have an enemy. His name is Satan. Satan has an army of imps, demons under his command that cause hatred, bitterness, anger, lying, stealing, cheating, adultery, dishonest, family break-ups, and corruption. For every evil mentioned, there is a demon with that name. Their job is to destroy Christians and take as many to Hell with them as they can. John 10:10 says the thief comes to steal, kill, and destroy, but Christ comes to give everlasting life. The Bible says when we see Satan for who he really is, we will wonder why we should have had such fear. If we would apply God's word to our lives, believing greater is He that is in me than he that is in the world, and plant those mustard seeds of faith, we can be what God would have us to be. Watch out, mountain, God's soldier is coming through. The commander, Jesus Christ is leading the warfare. We are at war. We are in a spiritual battle. We can't see the enemy, but he is there. God has given us a map to salvation, and a plan to fight the enemy. God is now giving us our warfare armor.

We are soldiers for the army of God. We are in battle, and through Christ Jesus, we will not be defeated.

Ephesians 6:11: Put on the whole armor of God, that ye may be able to stand against the wiles of the devil.

We have to remember that the human being that we fight with is flesh and blood, and we do not wrestle with that, but we fight against principalities, rulers of darkness, and wickedness in high places.

Each one of these names is an officer in the army of Satan. These commanders have different imps under their rule, but God's word has given the Christian authority over the ruler of darkness and put the serpent under our feet. Let's stand tall and make our commander and chief proud of our works, as soldiers for the King of Kings. To glorify Jesus in our walk is my goal.

Okay, let's get ready. Already we're in boot camp. Trials, tribulations, and now God is giving us our orders. First, we must get ready for the enemy's blows. We must put on the full armor of God to stand against the evil.

I always start with my head. It's well to remember my pieces, my prayer: I put on the helmet of salvation to protect my mind from the wiles of Satan. Then I put on the breastplate of righteousness, guarding my heart from destruction. I gird up my loins to protect my vital organs, then I pull out the sword of the Spirit, which is the Bible and teaches all truth. I shod my feet with the preparation of the gospel, taking the gospel into the highways and byways, bringing in the sheaves. Last, I take up the shield of faith, where Satan throws his ammunition. I will hide in Jesus behind the shield. He is my protector.

1) Put on the full armor of God. Remember, Satan walks as a roaring lion to devour whoever he can.

It's time to put your trust and faith in the power of God. Sometimes I repeat myself, why? Because to me, what God has said is important. Until we apply His instructions to our lives and live them, we are powerless.

The Christian life begins at the cross. The cross changes lives, and the blood of Jesus Christ is real. It destroys the power of Satan and his demons. Jesus' life was not in vain; His walk, the miracles, His suffering, His put-downs. He said if we follow Him, we will go through the same things. But be of good cheer, God has laid a map out to success. Warfare. My life has reflected so many wars, but I serve and overcome, and I stumble like my Jesus. Someday I will stand before Him, all by myself, and I long to hear Him say, "Welcome, thou good and faithful servant."

Stand firm with what you believe and when you have done all to stand, STAND. (II Timothy 2:3) As good soldiers, we are to endure hardness. (II Timothy 2:4.) God has chosen you to be a soldier of Jesus Christ. (II Timothy 2:11-12) If we are dead with Christ, we will live; if we suffer, we will reign with Him. If we deny Him, He will deny us.

Now that we are equipped with our armor and in the uniform of the living God, let's get our ammunition in order. We are at war. We can't always see the enemy, but we know he's at work to destroy as John 10:10 says, but Jesus Christ gives us life. It's time to get beyond fear and get into faith. Faith is believing what God says and believing the word of God is truth. Roman 12:3 says God has dealt to each one of us a measure of faith. Faith is an everyday event; faith is knowing the chair you sat in will hold you up. Walking up and down stairs, knowing you've made it before you can make it again, this is the same kind of faith God wants us to have in everyday living. Know who we are in Jesus Christ, and no matter what happens, nothing can sway us from the job we have as soldiers of Jesus Christ. Everyone has faith. It's what we do with it, and how we use it, that matters. So come with me and jump into Romans 10:17: Faith comes by hearing, and hearing by the word of God. We become stronger in God when we apply belief to our hearts. God can do through us only what we allow. As we devour the word of God, more faith will arise in our souls, and our strength will burst open and nothing will stop us from achieving God's best for us.

Right now I'm reminded of a church member whose friend became suicidal. She lived about 40-plus miles from me. Beth asked me if I would go to her friend. She needed deliverance. Beth had talked to someone who was supposed to have a straight line to Heaven. He told her, "You must pray for three days before you do this, out of fear." Beth would not go.

I said, "You pray three days, but this can't wait. This is God's call, and she could die."

Jolyn took a day off work and we found this person's house. The deliverance went very well. Later, the calls came of "thank you," and "praise to God for His unfailing love." Her life was changed because action was taken. If God has given an assignment for us to do, we can pray and go, sending the Holy Spirit ahead to open doors to use us and speak through us. God is still on the throne, and Jesus said He would never leave us nor forsake us. When Beth heard the results of her friend's help, she felt like she had egg on her face. She had listened to a person who was used by Satan. If we had not heard God's call and went, would a life have been taken?

Warfare begins at the cross. Can you imagine the excitement of Satan and his demons when they witnessed the death of Jesus Christ? They thought their troubles were all over. Picture the partying around the cross when the imps thought they had destroyed the Christ Jesus.

The blood of Jesus pours from his body, and in the demon world screams are heard. What happens to the demons standing under the cross? The blood of Jesus falls on them and desolates the tormenting spirits. They no longer exist. Now the demons stop their dance and praise to their leader. They back away from Jesus. Fear penetrates them. They have seen the power of the blood of Jesus.

God told me, when you get into trouble or have problems, plead the blood of Jesus Christ. The blood is as powerful today as it was 2,000 years ago. Remember the warlock that was talking to my friend over the phone telling her to get out of deliverance and what he would do.

2) Plead the blood of Jesus Christ. When you are talking to God in your closet, close the ears, eyes, and mouth of Satan and his demons. Ask God to send His angels to get Satan and his demons so far away that they cannot hear, see, or speak. Then you are free to talk aloud, and what you say cannot be turned against you. Like it was with my son when he slit his wrists. You see, Satan can no longer know your thoughts. He is not your father. He can only act on your word.

3) Close the eyes, ears and mouths of Satan and his demons. Ask God to send His angels to send the demons far away so they can't hear or speak or see.

4) No matter what happens in our lives, it was all on the cross with Jesus. Thanking God in even the bad will bring out the good. What Satan means for evil, God will turn round for good. Read the book of Job. I love that book, and it was written for me, how about you? Job lost everything and was given so much more. When we thank God in our trials, He does something in us that no psychiatrist could ever do. As we are changing, so do our circumstances, and then God can truly use us.

Until we know what and how to do it, in all things give thanks, and God will turn the evil around for good.

Got enemies? Don't we all. I have found the Christians have been my worst enemies. I repeat myself: the only group that buries their wounded alive is the Christians. From the beginning of my salvation, I have had more problems with those calling themselves Christians than I have with the world. Again, we're not fighting against flesh and blood. I've been a dedicated, sold-out, God-loving, Jesus-bought Christian for over 37 years. I've had pastors from the pulpit tell their congregation to stay away from me. I've seen pastors drop dead, lose their churches, etc. God's word says to do his prophets no harm. I'm in obedience to what God's word says. He says in everything give thanks. Thank You, God, that pastors and lay people come against me, but You change that. Thank You, in the fact that I have enemies, but You take care of that, for You have said vengeance is Yours. I pray blessings on my enemies and let go and let God

I am in obedience to do what God's word tells me. How about you?

5) Thank You, God, in that I have enemies. I ask Your blessings on them for vengeance is Yours.

A part of warfare in my life is the Lord's Prayer. I shared how Satan tried to kill us while Mother was driving. The gas was pressed to the floor, it was a battle to keep the steering wheel in control, and the ditch and trees were coming up fast. Mother said to say the Lord's Prayer with her, and the gas was released and the steering wheel was free. Our lives were saved.

I told you about Billy and how this five-year-old was sick and dying, and saying the Lord's Prayer allowed pain-free sleep to come. These are simple truths that are not practiced as much as they should be. It's all in the words of our mouths.

Father in Heaven, I hold Your name high above all names, and Your works in my life.

Forgive me of my sins as I forgive those who sin against me. Protect me from temptations and evil.

Break forth Your reign in the hearts of others, and complete Your work on Earth.

Matthew 6:9-13: Our Father in Heaven hallowed be your name, your kingdom come, your will be done on earth as it is in Heaven. Give us this day our daily bread. Forgive us our debts, lead us not into temptation, but deliver us from evil, for thine is the Kingdom and the Power forever.

You want to be powerful Christian? You want to grow spiritually? This is the warfare I use. I'm no longer in boot camp. From my childhood until now, I have battled and still do. I am no longer a novice. I'm building steps to get to the plateau where God can fully use me. I'm now a soldier in God's army. Uncle Sam pointed a finger and said he wanted you. God says to you He wants you. So why not get equipped and join the service of God? It will count for eternity. Let's go over the warfare duties and commands to winning spiritual war.

1. (Ephesians 6) put on the full armor of God.
2. Plead the blood of Jesus Christ, over and through the situation.
3. Close the ears, eyes, and mouth of Satan and his demons. Send the angels of God to get Satan and his demons so far away they cannot hear, see or speak.
4. In everything give thanks, this will turn evil to good.
5. When you pray, ask blessings upon your enemies, thanking God for them, letting go letting God, for vengeance is God's.

6. Send out warring angels to do battle against the devil and demons and those opposing God's work

Let me tell you about a very dear friend of mine. I counseled many times with this battered woman. Her husband abused her terribly. I told her the next time he did, tell God to send His angels to close the ears, eyes and mouth of Satan and his demons.

She said, "If I do that, he would kill me."

Then God said if you can't do it verbally, do it in your mind. She said their horse donkey had gotten out and they tried to put the animal in the barn without success. Her two children and husband were spread out, and she was in the center. The animal charged at her and she couldn't move for fear. There was fire and anger in the animal's eyes. She didn't dare speak aloud, but in her mind she said, *God, send Your angels to get Satan and his demons out.* The wild animal stopped with dust flying, looked Carolyn in the eyes, turned around and walked into the barn. Greater is He who is in you, than he who is in the world.

I shared this same power with another person while her husband was beating her. She hollered out, "God, send your angels to get Satan and his demons out of here. Satan, you do not have power over me." Her husband weakened and fell to the floor, with no strength to get up, and she got away. Later, he told her never to do that to him again.

You've got the power. Use it.

Faith moves the hand of God. So by faith, put on your armor, ready your ammunition, stand tall, soldier, and Satan's army will know you, fear you, and God will receive the glory.

Let not your heart be troubled. If God is for you, who can be against you?

CHAPTER 14

APPALACHIAN MOUNTAINS

In 1989, God spoke to me to collect clothes. I know the voice of God and I obeyed. My basement and garage filled up. I didn't know where this stuff was going. Boxes were to the ceiling, filled and ready to go to wherever God's destination was. I could no longer move around in my basement. I only had a pathway to my washer and dryer. I thought I would have a breakdown. Then God spoke to me, to go see a man in town who had an empty building.

He said, "Anything for God." He took me in the upstairs, and when the door was opened, I saw windows from the south and west. I had flashbacks of dreams I had had for 15-20 years of this same room, where I was sorting clothes. I cashed in my life insurance in and bought this building, a church, and a mountain in the Appalachian Mountains, where we feed and clothe people and help to furnish homes. We needed people to volunteer their time and building supplies to get this church ready for services and for mission give-away.

Each week, I'm told of someone committing suicide in this area, and for two years people have been begging us to start services. We were told of a family living in this hollow where the church is, who only had cornmeal gravy for every meal. The boy told his mommy that God didn't even care, until God's Mission Outreach was able to get food boxes to this family. Their lives are totally changed because of the love of God reaching out through this ministry. At the time we had gotten to this family, Grandma was suicidal, her husband died, and her two sons were killed. Today, this same person is helping people from her porch and giving away from the church. She was given new clothes and attends a church a distance from her. Her granddaughter's grades have improved since she has been given new clothes, shoes, etc. Their self-esteem is being built up and the girl is now tenth highest in her class and is planning to go to nursing school on scholarships. That's what love does.

People volunteered finances, trucks, and trailers to get this stuff to my people in the mountains. From my parents' estate, I got $5,000 and bought a 26-foot covered truck to transport food, clothes, furniture, and miscellaneous items to the mountains. When the coal mines dissolved, it left people without money to move out and many of these dear souls have come from generations of families who have made the beautiful mountains their homes.

The Southern Appalachian community was established in 1750, and many families migrated to this new world by boat, seeking freedom from persecution by the crown in England and Europe. Orphans, people who could not pay their debts, all who were outcasts and criminals were put on boats.

These migrants cleared forests, built homes, and were taught by the Cherokee Indians to plant corn, potatoes, squash, beans, and tobacco. They were taught to hunt animals for meat and use the skins for clothing and blankets. Marriages were developed with both cultures.

The land was given to the settlers by the crown. Later, this land was taken over by lumbering and coal mining.

At one time, the coal mines flourished. The people had jobs and their needs were met. When the coal mines closed, it left people in poverty. Generations have called these mountains home and now they have no money to move and no place to go. These forgotten people are left where they are, many unable to work. Black lung, cancer, and suicides are common. Some have no beds. Blankets are a must, heating stoves are needed. We found a wood stove for a World War II vet. When he saw his stove, he petted it like it was a dog. With tears he kept saying, "We're going to be warm, we're going to be warm."

There are so many stories. I think of the missionaries visiting a family, asking for a drink of water and getting it in a tin can. A lady saw a stack of hankies and asked for them. She said they couldn't afford toilet paper, and she would use the hankies for her family like toilet paper and wash them to reuse them.

There are many missions and churches that misuse the people, charging for food that was given freely, putting themselves above those crying out for help. When we found out that groups we had worked with and helped were doing this same thing, we dropped them. We hear the cries of the hungry babies and children and the elderly who live in the slums and have very little income. We reach out the best we can, but we need the help of others.

After speaking in a church in Texas, God gave me a vision of Jesus sitting on a mountain, surrounded by the most beautiful blue haze. Later that same color was seen in the mountain. There was a valley, with 7 block white flat-top roof houses. Jesus had blue and white on, and held a big piece of slate in the air above his head, with a small outline of His face. To the left was a huge pine tree. I told this vision to the pastor. When we went to a convention, the Bishop gave a message on all the colors God showed me in the vision. I asked the Bishop if he had ever given this message before, and he said no! That was when I knew this vision was for me. Then it hit me: people were dying and going to Hell. Oh! God, bring in the workers. Souls need to be rescued, restored, and saved.

When I got back from my Appalachian trip, someone had brought in a picture of Jesus; just the paper, no frame. When I saw it, my spirit attached to this picture. I asked God what He was trying to tell me. I took it home to my computer room, hung it on the door, and sat asking God to show me what He wanted me to know. Nothing.

Adam came to visit. I showed him the picture I had drawn and told him God was linking this picture to the one in my office. He took my artwork, looking at the picture of Jesus over Jerusalem. Within a minute, he said, "Turn the flat-top houses along with Jesus, until you have just the small part of his face as shown in your drawing."

What an amazing thing. It was the same picture, only Jesus was looking over the Appalachian Mountains. We had looked all over for the same vision and got nowhere fast. Adam and Melda said the mountain we had bought was the mountain in the vision God gave. I disagreed, until the top of the mountain was cleared of all its shrubs and small trees. When I went up to the mountain, I saw the big pine tree to the left of us and I knew this was the place of my vision. My goal is to build a retreat for people to get away, to share the love of Jesus, and just reach out, building up the broken down in spirit, mind, and body. Everyone is important, and everyone needs to know it.

I believe all the things I've gone through as a child, my marriage, my children, all the rejections in my life, and the occult activities, are only stepping stones to the plateau God has for me. I know being in the mountains is ordained of God. I can relate to their hurts. I'm able to minister to those in the occult and to the witches who actively believe they are right in what they do. When the first settlers came, they brought old wives' tales and occult practices, and have passed their beliefs down from one generation to another. I believe it's time to set the captive free.

My heart's desire is to help those whom no one wants. We need help fixing up homes. We need building supplies, food, and finances. Anyone who would care to come aboard with me, you can write:

> God's Mission Outreach
> 110 Main Street
> Box 302
> Maple Rapids, Michigan 48853
> Ph: 989-682-4564

No, I was not born in the mountains. I was born in Michigan. My heart is so full of love for these people, many in the same kind of life I've lived. God opened the doors to go to these people. He spoke to me when I didn't know anything about the Appalachian Mountain people. He planted in me a mustard seed of faith that has grown into a big tree of life, branching out, touching the hurts and demonstrating the love of Jesus.

Matthew 25:32-46: Jesus said, "I was hungry, and you fed me. Thirsty, and you gave me drink. I was a stranger and you invited me in. In prison, and you visited me."

"When, Lord, did I do this?"

"When you did it to these brothers, you did it for me."

When God told me to collect clothes and then to go to the mountains, He said, "You feed and clothe these people, and they will come to Me." We see this happening. We just need helpers with the heart of Jesus in this field that is ready for the harvest.

Luke 10:30: Bandits robbed, stripped and beat a traveler, leaving him for dead. A Jewish Priest saw this man in need of help and passed him by. A Levite also passed him by. But a Samaritan, despised by the Jews, stopped and helped. He took the man upon his donkey to a nearby inn. He gave the innkeeper money to pay for a room and the injured man's care, and if more was needed, he would pay the bill. These men of the cloth passed by a man in need. What about the church today? Are they not passing by the hunger and needs of those crying to God for help? What kind of neighbors are we? Which one of the characters do we identify with? We need to make our lives count, and reach beyond self.

The church has lost its power because they have not put God first. Jesus said, "Feed my sheep." Jesus said go to the highways and bring them in. The harvest is ready, but where are the laborers?

What we sow, we will reap.

I have used all my money, cashing in my life insurance to help the Appalachian Mountain people. With that money, I bought a mountain, where God gave me a vision of Jesus sitting on a mountain, holding a big piece of slate in his hands, and below that mountain, eight white block homes. I believe God wants a building on top of the mountain to bring pastors, lay people, and those in need of God's love, to teach them, with the eight buildings for dorms, making a difference in the life of those involved, showing the true love of God, and seeing lives change for the kingdom of God. Pray with us that someone will hear the cries of the less fortunate, those who have been forgotten, and build in those who feel no one cares. God cares – do you?

CHAPTER 15

GOD'S PROMISES

Remember, my mother was a child herself when she brought me into the world. I look back at her strength and courage in raising two young children, and taking care of her parents while Daddy served in World War II so we could be free. These men and women gave their lives in the war. I'm so proud of my father and those who serve to make us free.

My father's life on the front lines and in the Battle of the Bulge did not free him, but imprisoned him in a man-made, self-contained Jekyl and Hyde personality. The battle never eliminates memories, it only creates flashbacks and horrors that people try to drown out with drugs and drinking and other addictions.

Dad's drinking caused fights between him and Mother. I remember Dad pushing Mother through a window. Her arms were all cut up, yet she stayed. She had children, and they were important to her.

When Mom and Dad moved to Florida, they did a lot of fishing and flea markets and the first few years were very good. Even though Dad didn't drink, he had some alcoholic ways. He was a controller, and one time, Mother told me she wasn't living, only existing. My heart broke for her. She was isolated from her children and only at Christmas did my children and I get to Florida to see her.

Mother had very little company. She cooked and cleaned, and Dad had a fit if she watched TV. One day Dad came into the house and found the pots burning on the stove and Mother was slurring her words. She had had a stroke. She had lung cancer that went to her brain. I got a call on the day I was having surgery, to tell me Mother would have a tumor removed from her brain. There was no way I could get to her in time. Mother finally told me she was being abused, and my brother and I went to her, leaving on my birthday. Mother said I was her angel and protector, and I did all I could. These two months of caring for Mother was like a gift.

Mother was being given chemotherapy treatments, and with every treatment I saw her health fail. I did everything I knew to do. I knew she was dying and we needed some spiritual help, so I called their pastor. He was too tired, he had worked in the garden and couldn't come. I cried out to God: We need help. What do I do? The thought came to me to call the talk show that sells products for the listener. I did, and I asked if there was any pastor that could visit my mother and to help my dad through this horrible time. Three pastors came over, and one really struck a cord with my dad. Thank You, Jesus. It might have been two weeks later that Mother got real bad. I was in her room with her, and her eyes would search the room as though she was seeing something.

"Mother, are you seeing angels?"

"I'm seeing something," she said, and a short time later she passed away.

I know she is in Heaven, waiting. I had the privilege of leading her to the Lord.

I remembered when I was about nine years old and I got into poison ivy and sumac. My leg began to rot, and the stench was bad. Mother put bread and milk poultices on it to draw the poisons out. The doctor had talked about cutting my leg off, and we were pleased to see the healing. I still have the scars there, as a reminder of Mother's quick thinking.

Now and again I have flashbacks to those painful days of my childhood, and I cry. I feel bad Mother had to suffer as she did. But at least I was able to capture good memories, too.

Mother, like her parents, loved flowers. I guess I follow in their footsteps. I tried to find blue morning glory seeds, without success. My son had some pink flowers, and I decided those were better than none. I planted them, and the next year we had morning glories like you wouldn't believe. The flowers were blue on the inside, and when they closed up, they were pink on the outside. God said He would give me the desires of my heart.

Someone donated a van to the mission, and the only place to park it at the mission was under the long branches of a black walnut tree, maybe 50 years old. Sap and nuts would drop and hit the van. I said I needed to talk to the neighbors, to see if these branches could be cut. Within two weeks, when I went to park the van, something looked different. At first I couldn't tell what, and then I noticed the branches were all cut off. Within another week, the tree was down. I didn't say anything to Max, the neighbor, only to God, and it was done.

I love the Lord so much. I asked God one time, why did my heart have so much love for others? He answered: "Because you know. You've been there."

All proceeds from this book will go towards God's Mission Outreach and the Appalachian Mountains.

100% of everything given to the mission is freely given to the people.

Come go with us…

> God's Mission Outreach
> 110 Main Street
> Box 302
> Maple Rapids, Michigan 48853
> Ph: 989-682-4564

www.ingramcontent.com/pod-product-compliance
Ingram Content Group UK Ltd.
Pitfield, Milton Keynes, MK11 3LW, UK
UKHW041954230426
12048UKWH00008B/334